If you don't like the war,
switch the damn thing off!

# If you don't like the war, switch the damn thing off!

## Jack Cahill

with photographs by the author

Musson Book Company
a division of General Publishing Co. Limited
Don Mills, Ontario

First published in 1980 by
Musson Book Company
30 Lesmill Road, Don Mills, Ontario

First printing

Canadian Cataloguing in Publication Data
Cahill, Jack.
If you don't like the war,
switch the damn thing off!
ISBN 0-7737-0043-9
1. Vietnamese Conflict, 1961-1975 – Personal narratives, Canadian.
2. Vietnamese Conflict, 1961-1975 – Journalists.   3. Cahill, Jack.
I. Title
DS559.5.C35   959.704'38   C80-094014-8

Jacket design/Robin Taviner

Passage on pages 70-71 reprinted by permission of The Associated Press;
on pages 106-110 by permission of United Press International.

Passage on pages 87-88 from *Murder of a Gentle Land* by John Barron
and Anthony Paul, New York: Reader's Digest Press. 1977. Reprinted by
permission of McGraw-Hill Book Company.

Printed and bound in Canada
ISBN O-7737-0043-9

To Marie

# Contents

# Acknowledgments

A foreign correspondent can't function without friends. He needs the advice of his colleagues. He needs their company, especially on the difficult or dangerous assignments. And the friends he makes in these circumstances are the best of all.

Many such friends helped me write this book either by becoming characters in it or by refreshing my memory on events and anecdotes. When we meet again, wherever the crisis is, I owe a lead on a story or a lift "down the road" particularly to Neil Davis, the correspondents' correspondent, who now works for NBC out of Bangkok; Tony Paul, my old Australian colleague who is the roving editor for *Readers' Digest* in Asia; Peter Arnett of Associated Press, Pulitzer Prize winner and veteran of the Vietnam War; Brian Ellis, former Saigon bureau chief and now foreign editor of CBS Television News in New York; Bill Stewart of *Time* magazine; Peter Kent and Ian Wilson who are now covering Africa for NBC and the Canadian Broadcasting Corporation; Colin Hoath, who was my

CBC colleague for most of my years in Hong Kong; and Mike Best, my thoroughly professional deskmate at *The Toronto Star*, who commented on the manuscript as it came from the typewriter.

A foreign correspondent also can't function without good editors. I have been fortunate to have at least three of them, Geoff Stevenson and John Miller, foreign editors of the *Star* during most of my time abroad, and Julie Beddoes who encouraged and edited the book.

# Introduction

From all over the world the correspondents are being called home. Bush jackets, with their big, practical, notebook-sized pockets that button down to deter the alley thieves of every continent, are being hung, some with sadness and some with relief, in the closets of comfortable homes in London, Washington, Berlin, and Toronto.

One reason is the home newspapers' economising, another is isolationist ignorance. As modern communications technologies quickly shrink a world whose countries are increasingly interdependent, paradoxically the Western news media are turning from the global reality to a narrow localism that is supposed to sell papers or attract viewers. When the West had had enough of bad news from the Asian wars, it simply switched them off.

The foreign correspondent's life is dangerous. The old hands had it easier. When they covered wars they covered one side of them with all the protection and logistic support of a friendly army. But now they

11

report on two sides and often both are unfriendly. The contact in the field is no longer a helpful G.I. or cool British officer but an excited, uneducated, fifteen-year-old kid, carrying all the authority of an automatic weapon, often bigger than he is. And the head of state to be interviewed is often an illogical dictator who is convinced that the Western correspondent is part of a "Zionist plot" and respects him somewhat less than he does the scores of his own countrymen he has had killed in his rise to power.

In the circumstances there is not much ambition any more among younger newsmen to become foreign correspondents. It is comfortable at home. The journalism schools are producing kids who want to be drama critics or instant editors, and few opt these days to begin on the police beat which might lead them eventually into the wider, real world.

Consequently, their judgments, when they come to positions of power in the press, tend to be as narrow as their experience. Readers and viewers, they say, are not interested in world affairs but in local issues. They are wrong, of course. The streets of my own city of Toronto teem these days with people from everywhere, from India and Pakistan, China and Vietnam, Guyana and Lebanon, and it is the same in all major Western cities. While those who control the Western media retreat from the world, the world is chasing after them. And in the meantime we are creating an information vacuum as eerie as the empty villages of Vietnam, abandoned when the hasty retreat outpaced the inevitable advance at the end of the war.

A survey carried out by the Overseas Press Club of America shows that in 1975 there were 429 full-time American correspondents working abroad. This includes radio and TV technicians as well as on-air correspondents and the writing press. At that time the news organizations employed another 247 non-

12

American staffers abroad. Three years earlier the total had been 797, and in 1969, when the Vietnam war was at its height, there were 929. The decline has been more rapid since the survey.

The Canadian media have never done much of a job of reflecting the world to their audience, even though the Canadian correspondent has an advantage over his colleagues in that he is regarded as a reflection of his country: honest, fair, and comparatively harmless, but with close links to the big powers and therefore potentially influential. Canada is also a massive donor of foreign aid, which does no harm at all to the journalist anxious for access to a closed country or an interview with a head of state.

But in Canada, only my paper, *The Toronto Star*, and *The Globe and Mail*, also from Toronto and which has concentrated its foreign coverage largely on Peking, have shown any real direct interest in foreign affairs over the years. The Canadian Broadcasting Corporation and Southam New Services have maintained a small number of excellent and usually overworked correspondents abroad. All are retrenching.

Many of the young deskmen in newspaper offices at home have taken lately to wearing neatly pressed and definitely undusty bush jackets as a sort of summer uniform. Their bureaucratic ambitions often exceed their journalistic abilities. The news is not much more than a piece of paper that arrives on their desks already edited by the few U.S. papers that still operate full foreign news services. And how it got there, the problems, the risks, the professionalism and dedication of the foreign correspondents who produced it, is beyond their understanding.

Ernest Hemingway was one of *The Toronto Star's* first foreign correspondents and Gordon Sinclair took an occasional colorful look at the wider world. Gregory Clark filed much of his wonderful whimsy from abroad. Since then many distinguished Canadian journalists, including the scholarly Mark Gayn, have done their best stories far from the comforts of home and the ease of covering city hall. Clark, the pixyish World War Two correspondent, who was probably the best writer of all, might have been anticipating today's return to deskbound journalism when he strode angrily into the newsroom one day and faced the editor who had dared to alter his copy.

"Listen, my fellow," he told the deskman-editor, "we are the hunters. We go out into the fields and the forests and we bring back the golden pheasants. But you, you son of a bitch, are a scullery maid."

Gregory Clark would be appalled now as the foreign news business deteriorates into a mess of middle management, accounting judgments, dependency on American or British bias; and at the danger of information management by the CIA, the KGB, and all the other governments waging their propaganda wars.

Clark's golden pheasant is fatter than ever these days, out there in the far and adventurous fields and forests. But the hunters, unfortunately, are few now and the chiefs in their comfortable offices generally uninterested.

## CHAPTER 1

# How we came to be in the East

I met Marie when I was a reporter on the police beat in Sydney, Australia, and she was pulling the bullets out of the bodies of people I had to write about. She was the prettiest nurse in the casualty ward of St. Vincent's Hospital, in the then wild, central-city area of King's Cross. She was also my worst contact because she steadfastly refused to tell me anything about the characters in her care even after we decided we'd be married. She was a good nurse and she is the best wife in the world.

We had decided to move, temporarily we thought, from Sydney to Vancouver shortly after we were married in 1956, mainly because it was hard to find a decent house or apartment in Sydney in those days and also because the Sydney *Daily Telegraph*, for which I was the chief crime reporter, was having some industrial troubles. As well, the publisher of the Vancouver *Sun*, during a visit to Australia, had made a vague, unwritten offer of a job if I ever wanted to pay my own way over.

This cost of making our own move was a problem, however. I was one of the top-paid reporters in what was then a highly competitive newspaper city and one of the youngest, at twenty-four, ever to be graded an A-plus journalist under the very effective Australian system which ranks reporters and editors according to their ability and experience and provides substantial merit pay for the top grades. But I put much of the money in the poker machines at the Journalists' Club in the small hours of the morning when the city was dead. And Marie, who didn't work after we were married, likes expensive things.

But the stupidity of the bureaucracy came to our rescue by providing the cash for our one-way fare in a strange way. It takes some explaining:

Apart from my police beat duties in those days I used to do what we jokingly called "reporting in depth."

It was the beginning of the scuba diving era. Jacques Cousteau's books were opening to sea-loving Australians the wonders of the underwater world and a small group of enthusiasts, led by Don Linklater of Bondi Beach, had even designed and built its own aqualungs after the Cousteau pattern.

When the city was comparatively quiet one night I was given an assignment to interview these madmen who were diving in their home-made gear down among the sharks off the rugged, surf-beaten coast, and they intrigued me with stories of their adventures and particularly with their determination to make their deepest dive, and establish an Australian depth record, in a few weeks' time.

"Why don't you come down with us to cover the story?" Linklater asked, jokingly, I think. "We'll give you a training dive next week."

Four of us did the dive in the ocean outside Sydney Harbor a few weeks later, plunging down through a confusion of colorful fish and the shadows of a few sharks to a depth of 118 feet, not deep at all in comparison with today's diving records, but it was as far as we could go without digging a hole in the sandy continental shelf. And, because we considered ourselves to be the only aqualung divers in Australia and New Zealand, we declared this effort to be the Australasian depth diving record. It made a good story and the "record" actually held up for a year or two until some proper equipment was imported to replace our homemade stuff.

This story led to many other adventures and reports along the Australian coast. We studied sharks and why they attacked people. We found some of the oldest wrecks and salvaged artifacts that are still star exhibits at the Sydney Museum. And, for a stunt, when there were shark scares off the Sydney beaches, I used to dive in Sydney Harbor, grab a shark by the tail and "aquaplane" behind it while a diver took pictures with the only homemade underwater camera in Australia.

The trick was to grab the tail of a variety known as the Port Jackson shark, which looks as vicious as any other, but in fact must be the laziest and dumbest of all underwater creatures. It also has no teeth.

I was quite frank about all this, but in shark-scared Sydney nobody would believe there was such a thing as a harmless, frightened, toothless shark, and the *Telegraph* would gleefully print front-page pictures of me virtually pushing a poor old Port Jackson through the water adjacent to pictures of crowds fleeing the beaches in fear of the fins of a really deadly Gray Nurse, or Tiger, or Hammerhead.

In turn all of this led to a major magazine assignment: go to Rabaul in New Britian, an island north of New Guinea, the site of some of the worst air-sea battles of World War II. Explore some of the hundreds of battleships, submarines and merchant ships on the bottom of Rabaul Harbor. We want a big takeout on how the relics of war look on the tenth anniversary of peace in the Pacific. Take your crazy photographer friend who shoots you with the sharks and tell him this time we want color.

Frank Packer, later Sir Frank, who owned the *Telegraph*, and who mounted the early Australian challenges for the Americas Cup yacht races, was bringing out a new magazine, it was explained, and we were expected to provide the first cover story. Obviously this was an expensive undertaking. We had to ship half a dozen aqualungs and our own compressed air along with photographic equipment and ourselves to Rabaul, about 3,000 miles away. We also had to rent boats and crews.

But at the same time Packer was on one of his notorious economy campaigns: walk a block from the office to save a penny section fare in the tram; use half a piece of copy paper for short stories. And most of all, no entertainment expense whatever, for any purpose, at any time, on any story.

When I got off the old Sunderland flying boat in Rabaul, a village of native huts, a few houses on stilts, and a small hotel, with a French businessman who doubled as the "mad" underwater photographer, I asked where we could rent some boats. I was told a man named John Chipper, an Australian who had made a fortune from the scrap metal of war, had a small fleet.

"Hell, take them," Chipper said when I asked what the cost would be. "I don't need them at present. You can have the yacht and the tug. It will do the crews good to have some work to do. You don't have to pay for them. Take me to dinner after you've got your story."

We used the boats for four weeks, got some good underwater pictures of sunken submarines and bat-

18

tleships, their coral-encrusted guns pointing skywards, their cabins and holds inhabited by huge grouper or schools of deadly yellow and black striped water snakes, and we heard from Sydney that the quality was good and we had, in fact, made the magazine cover.

So on the night before we left Rabaul we took Chipper to the only place in the village that served a steak and a bottle of Australian wine. We thanked him profusely for the boats. The evening cost me exactly twenty Australian pounds. And when we got back to Sydney, somewhat pleased with our success, I put in my expense account, a big one, including: "For entertaining John Chipper, who loaned a luxury yacht with a crew of three and a tug with a crew of five [I didn't mention most of them were New Britian natives who were paid at that time about five shillings a month] for four weeks—twenty pounds."

I thought some common sense would overcome the no entertainment rule, but I overestimated, as I often have since, the ability of a bureaucracy to adjust to reality. The accountants rejected the twenty pound claim. I stormed into the office of King Watson, the editor of the *Telegraph*, complaining about the stupidity of accountants and the unreality of ivory tower rules, and I insisted, at the end of the one-way conversation that he, the editor, should tell Packer, the publisher, to use the cover of his new magazine to wipe a part of his anatomy.

Watson, one of the great editors, was never fazed by anything or anybody, especially angry young reporters, and he just sat there behind his big desk, leaning back in his swivel chair, grinning. "You're a young man," he said after a while, "but you're a senior reporter and you've been in this game long enough to know about accountants.

"What you must do is obvious," he advised. "You must put down for *hiring* the damn boats. Then the

19

stupid bastards will approve it. Then you will get out of my hair and let me bring out a newspaper."

"But," I said, "King, even the dumbest accountant knows you can't hire a tug and a yacht and their crews for a month for twenty lousy pounds."

"Here," he said. "Give it to me."

He grabbed the expense account, altered the word loaned to hired and the twenty-pound charge to 420.

"The stupid bastards will pass that," he said. "And Packer deserves it."

Four hundred pounds was a lot of money in those days, more than two month's salary. It paid our fare by ship to Canada, with a little left over.

I covered crime for the Vancouver *Sun* until I was promoted to cover British Columbian provincial politics. Provincial politics led to national and in 1962 I went to Ottawa as bureau chief, first for the *Sun*, then for *The Toronto Star*, Canada's largest daily newspaper. I've worked for the *Star* ever since.

We stayed in Ottawa during the hectic decade of the Pearson years, with their crisis a day, the scandals, the flag debate, the new Canadian nationalism, the beginning of the Trudeau years, and the Quebec crisis of 1970. I remember the long gray night in October when I watched from my office on Wellington Street for the lights to go out in the East Block of the Parliament buildings. This would announce that the decision had been made whether or not to declare a state of emergency. Suddenly there were troops in battledress in the streets of Ottawa, guns around the Peace Tower, soldiers storming into Parliament buildings carrying automatic weapons.

I watched three prime ministers. I remember the day we wrote a story stating: "Prime Minister Lester Pearson today warned his cabinet that further leaks to the press from cabinet meetings would not be tolerated." Somebody had leaked us the story.

Several years later I sat under a tree at Tamerlane's grave in Samarkand, deep in the Soviet Union, with a frightened bride named Margaret Trudeau, trying to convince her she should not be afraid of the cameramen and publicity. "I'm shy," she said. "I'm a private person. I just want to be Pierre's wife." She changed.

It was during my Ottawa-based years that I met my only real, semicovert, Canadian spook—a spy. He was a second secretary in Moscow in the late sixties during the visit to Russia of a former prime minister, the late John Diefenbaker.

The *Star* sent me on this job, I assume, because Diefenbaker, the Chief, who was even then supposed to be in his dotage, was expected to make a fool of himself. He proved everyone wrong. He did go about the Ukraine emulating De Gaulle's gaffe in Montreal in 1967 by shouting, in effect, *"Vive l'Ukraine libre!"* much to the embarassment of the Canadian embassy and his Soviet hosts, but he was no fool. He knew exactly what he was doing.

The Diefenbaker party was assigned the young second secretary from the Canadian embassy as adviser and protector. He spoke fluent Russian, had just had his driver's license revoked, which was usually the first move toward expulsion, and was fairly frank most of the time about the real nature of his duties in Moscow.

His Soviet counterpart on the trip was Rita, a serious, woman in her early thirties, allegedly from Intourist but obviously an agent, and the two of them got along famously together, like a couple of opposition journalists on the same story, linked by the bond of their profession, but rivals at the same time.

On our last night in the Ukraine they were both considerably relieved that Diefenbaker, although he had been difficult, had not done anything to upset the balance of power in the world, and they celebrated by

21

relaxing at the Kiev Hotel's regular Saturday night dinner dance with its corny, old Western music. The two young spooks joined us at our table. They indicated that this was to be a night for relaxation by moving both the vase of flowers and the little Canadian flag from the table, and presumably the bugs with them. It was quite touching the way they did this. First the Canadian moved the flag and then the Russian girl smiled broadly, picked up the flowers and moved them to a buffet far away. Even spooks need a Saturday night off, especially after a tough job.

They danced together until the early hours of the morning and by the end of the evening seemed quite fond of each other, were frank about their real activities and were openly discussing the problems and techniques associated with them.

I told the Canadian I thought I'd write a color story about this touching professional bonhomie and he had no objections, but next day when I tried to file it with Reuters Moscow bureau, where you have to punch your own copy on the teletype machine, the machine broke down as soon as the word "spy" left the teletype keys.

"The KGB will be watching and you've sent them into a tizzy," the Reuters bureau chief explained. "They'll have a committee meeting about it. And then they might let it through just to see what else it says."

After twenty-five attempts when the machine broke down at the first mention of the word spy, the story did go through. It caused considerable embarassment at the Canadian embassy where they seemed to know about it almost immediately. And I was followed by a phalanx of KGB men until, with great relief, I boarded an Air Canada plane for Montreal the next day.

Diefenbaker, who obviously knew all about the story and the reason for our large number of shadowy followers, never made any direct mention of it, except to say as we flew somewhere near Stockholm: "It's so good to breathe the freedom. And I hear you were a naughty boy. Good for you."

He never failed to send me a Christmas card until his death, often with a little scrawl stating, "Remember Russia."

The spy story arrived in Toronto intact, but never appeared in the *Star* and shortly after I got home I was debriefed at great length on the incident by a friendly RCMP sergeant over lunch. And that seemed to be the end of it.

Diefenbaker ran well ahead of the clumsy Soviet spy system on that journey anyway. Not only did he not make a fool of himself, as many expected, he managed to use the Soviet intelligence apparatus for his own purposes.

Knowing his penchant for history, the Russians gave Diefenbaker the room in Moscow's National Hotel which had once been occupied by Lenin and from the balcony of which the great revolutionary addressed the masses in Red Square. A huge portrait of Lenin dominated the room and Diefenbaker, for some reason, was certain the bug was either behind the portrait or the portrait itself was some sort of television camera.

Consequently, every day at breakfast, he would announce to me, the only newsman on the tour, that he was going to have a press conference in his room at four o'clock that afternoon.

"For God's sake, Chief," I would tell him. "I don't want to have a press conference. Who needs it? I'm having breakfast with you, and lunch. Just tell me what you want to say."

"An official press conference, Jack," the old man would insist, wagging a finger. "At four o'clock in my room. Be there."

So at four o'clock sharp I would knock on his door and he would shout: "Is that Mr. Cahill of *The Toronto Star* and are you here for an official press conference? If so, come in."

Then, after I'd settled in a chair, he would turn to the picture of Lenin on the wall and shout: "Let's get the ground rules of this press conference straight first. Do you represent the biggest newspaper in Canada?"

"Indeed I do, Mr. Diefenbaker," I would admit.

"And how long will it take you to get your dispatch about the press conference to the people of Canada, Mr. Cahill," the old man would shout.

By this time, I too was almost yelling at Lenin's likeness.

"Maybe an hour, Mr. Len—er—Mr. Diefenbaker," I would reply.

"And what," Diefenbaker would ask, dropping his voice sonorously and wagging his jowls, "would be the reaction of the people of Canada if you wrote that I was not treated the way I should be by the Russian people?"

"Sir," I would shout at Lenin, "there might be riots in the streets."

"Well, Mr. Cahill," the old Chief would say. "I see you have your notebook there. I want you to take this down carefully. I would like to announce that I want to see Mr. Polyanski tomorrow. Have you written that down?"

"I have Mr. Diefenbaker," I would shout at Lenin. "I have written down in my notebook that you want to see Mr. Polyanski tomorrow."

"Good," Diefenbaker would then announce. "That is the end of the press conference."

Lenin, of course, may have been a completely innocent party to all this and the bug somewhere else in the room. The way Diefenbaker was shouting he could perhaps have been heard on the other side of the Red

24

Square. But the "press conferences" always worked. Next day Diefenbaker would receive an invitation to see Vice-Chairman Polyanski, or get whatever else it was he wanted.

She was slim and rather pretty and for someone who lived out of a small suitcase and spent much of her time war watching in the worst countries, her dress was just right for a dinner at Winston's, one of Toronto's most elegant restaurants. She was also charming, intelligent, attentive. She didn't say much. She listened a lot.

Georgie Ann Geyer, one of the best of the foreign correspondents, was doing her thing in a highly professional way for the old Chicago *Daily News*. Her assignment: Go up to Canada for a few days and do an in-depth piece on the 1972 federal election. As usual, a ridiculous hit and run assignment, but Georgie Ann had managed to pull off the main trick of her trade—to be in the right place at the right time. Somehow she had inveigled herself into, or been invited to, or for all I know somehow subtly organized, this dinner at Winston's at which Martin Goodman, Peter Regenstreif and I were to discuss the campaign, then in its final stages, and the possible outcome.

As chief of the *Star*'s Ottawa bureau, I had been on the election trail for months and information about the mood of the vast land and the chances of every candidate in all of the 264 ridings was flowing to me from our political staff, some of the best reporters in the business.

Goodman, an old hand at politics, had a balancing overview of all this as the *Star*'s managing editor, and Regenstreif, one of Canada's top political pollsters, had just compiled his final figures.

In the circumstances Georgie Ann had succeeded in her assignment even before Goodman had ordered

25

the second bottle of Chateau Neuf du Pape. In less than an hour she had absorbed the combined and, to the *Star*, expensive experiences of the three of us—enough to write a whole series of stories if she wanted to—and fortunately for her our predictions for that election were right on.

Then when the cognacs came, Goodman drew me aside from the others and changed the conversation. "What the hell are we going to do with you when the election is over?" he asked. "Your term in Ottawa is up. How would you like to go to Asia?"

I thought for maybe a second.

"OK," I told Goodman. "When?"

## CHAPTER 2

# I'm not good enough to be a Communist

Hong Kong was our home base during the years I was *The Toronto Star*'s Far Eastern correspondent.

Hong Kong is a crowd, a constant noise, a babble of bargaining, a sweatshop, a stock market, a gamble, a stink, a frightening big wind in the typhoon season.

Hong Kong is also the blue waters lapping into little peaceful coves, the view from Victoria Peak over the wide ocean, and the serenity of Chinese grandmothers, walking hand-in-hand with little well-dressed kids in the parks.

Hong Kong is the *Hakka* ladies, their backs temporarily and their legs permanently bent as they carry big loads of bricks in baskets on construction sites, and millionaire's wives in Paris originals at the symphony concerts at city hall. It is pink Rolls Royces and rickshaws, noodle stores in the streets next to elegant French restaurants, Buddhist temples and Catholic cathedrals, mansions surrounded by squatters' shacks, and sleek company yachts moored beside poor, unpainted, little junks on which big families live all their lives.

The people of Hong Kong worship the dollar. They also burn joss sticks in the streets and sweep the graves of their ancestors religiously every *Ching Ming* day. They build huge, modern, chrome and glass skyscrapers, then place mirrors on all of the windows to deflect the *fung shui*—the evil spirits.

Police station sergeants become millionaires from payoffs from the brothels and gambling joints. The firemen expect "tea money," often in substantial amounts, otherwise not only will they refuse to extinguish a fire in your home or business, they might start one. I had a few drinks one night with the British chief of the Royal Hong Kong Police Force's Triad (Chinese Mafia) squad and a BBC crew who were doing a documentary on him titled *Hong Kong's Honest Cop*. The next afternoon the honest cop was arrested for corruption.

Yet in Hong Kong the daughers of the *gweilos* (foreign devils) can walk anywhere, unmolested, at any time of the day or night.

You can buy anything in Hong Kong, if you have the money, from the oddest of sexual services to an air force of second-hand fighter planes. If you care to venture into the walled city of Kowloon, where the buildings are so tall and the muddy streets so narrow the light never reaches the ground, you can arrange to equip an army or shoot a fix into a million arms. But you shouldn't go there unless you are known to the street vendors outside the only two entrances. The throats of all unknowns, including policemen, are consistenly slit.

Hong Kong should not work, but it does. The thousands of refugees who pour over the border every year, seeking a better life among the five million people already crowded into four square miles, should not be able to find homes and jobs and a better life, but they do.

The deep ideological differences between the many Chinese in the colony who are still firm followers of the Maoist revolution, and the far-right British *Tai Pans*, their expatriate capitalist employees, the Chinese millionaires and the stockmarket gamblers, should cause riots in the streets, but they don't, or at least haven't since the Great Proletarian Cultural Revolution in 1967.

The question everybody asks about Hong Kong is: when will the mainland Chinese take it over? The answer is: yesterday. Much of the colony's water supply already comes from the mainland. So does much of its food and oil. The Chinese cross back and forth over the border with Kwangtung province on business or family matters almost at will. The Bank of China, with its quiet, swarming crowd of Mao-jacketed Communist cadres, helps dominate the downtown area, towering over the little central park, where until recently the British and Indians and Australians played cricket in their whites and colorful caps. The many journalists of the New China News Agency are all senior Communist cadres. The British still *administer* the little colony with supurb skill. But the Communists *control* it.

The British are constructing the world's most modern subway system in Hong Kong, making much noise in the downtown area, and incidentally making it necessary for the removal of the sacred cricket pitch. It is expensive and it may even be a successful subway system. More importantly it follows the Maoist instruction to "dig tunnels deep and store wheat," adding to the miles of underground defence areas under all major Chinese cities.

The Chinese big businessmen with their chauffered Mercedes or Rolls Royces—a few of them gold plated—their huge shipping lines and portfolios of some of the world's most expensive real estate, in Hong

Kong and abroad, manage to maintain remarkably adaptable dual loyalties, buttering their bread on both sides of the border, ignoring ideologies in their scramble for more and more money.

Ho Yin is an example of these businessmen. He operates mainly in the tiny neighboring allegedly Portuguese colony of Macao, which is a gambling joint, Asia's Las Vegas, an incongruous pimple of ultracapitalism on the rump of Communist China. Macao is even more under Communist control than is Hong Kong and only forty-five minutes away by fast, efficient, capitalist-operated hydrofoil services.

Ho Yin owns Macao's electricity company, the jai alai court and the dog track, among other things, including eleven cars and one of the world's richest collections of jade. He is also a respected member of the Communist People's Congress in Peking.

A colleague once asked Ho Yin, in a rare interview, how he could possibly reconcile all of his personal power and riches with communism.

"I'm not good enough to be a Communist," he replied

It was always good to get home to Hong Kong, especially from places like Cambodia and Vietnam. The aircraft aims straight at a big black and white square painted on a hill near Kai Tak airport, swerves suddenly through a ninety-degree turn and swoops frighteningly between tall apartment buildings, with the inevitable washing hanging from the balconies, until it bounces on the long runway. If it is not the most difficult landing in the world, it is at least the most exciting.

Sometimes, as the plane taxied along the strip that juts out into the "fragrant harbor" which gives the island its name, I could see through the window my own little sloop, moored safely among the junks and sampans at Kellett Island, where the *gweilos* sip their long, cool, drinks at the Royal Hong Kong Yacht Club, incongruously near to a huge cluster of ugly harbor tenders crowded with Chinese families who live on them, seldom stepping ashore.

Usually there was a period of impatience to get home as we drove a few blocks to the Cathay Pacific cargo hut to ship rolls of film to Canada, waiting while the clerk laboriously typed out the bill of lading in English, then demanded my Chinese "chop"—or signature—so it could be sent home collect.

The Chinese characters representing my Irish name on my carved ivory chop translated vaguely into "expectations of excellence." It worked. The film was always sent collect.

Then the big Mercedes taxi would crawl through the thick traffic of Kowloon, past the street stalls with their dead ducks hanging among the colorful plastics and clothing and the ivory carvings, past the pharmacies with their varieties of wines, from five-mice wine with the five little white pickled bodies in the bottle, to male silkworm sperm wine. Good, the label says, for impotence and nocturnal emissions. Then through the area of textile factories where the big guillotines cut huge piles of denim into jeans by the millions and little old ladies sew several different brand names onto products that pour from the same machines to fill the store shelves of the world.

The big car picked up speed in the tunnel under the harbor and slowed again on the Hong Kong side in the hustle and smell of narrow Queen Street, near the big People's Republic Store, where you can buy anything from the Mainland from works of art to cheap cashmere sweaters and frozen donkey legs; past the snake shops where the big, live cobras wait in wire cages to have their stomachs slit and their biles neatly squeezed into bowls of rice wine to make a concoction guaranteed to keep a Chinese warm all through a winter.

The way winds through the university area, a

bunch of buildings on either side of Pokfulam Road, and eventually up a big hill. We lived in a huge, old, white stucco house on a pocket of land carved out of a mountainside so steep it seemed to hover over the flat roof, ready to fall at any time. Once when I was in Malaysia the Canadian Commission had a somewhat panicky call from Marie saying it had done just that during a typhoon. In fact the mountain had only slid a bit against the back of the house near the maid's quarters, almost burying our maid in the process and sending the family scuttling to the Hilton Hotel for a few days.

The outside of the house was covered by an ugly, green, slimy fungus that grows long and lush in the high humidity, but inside it was palatial, built in 1946 by a Chinese millionaire for his bride, a mausoleum of rich wood, winding staircases, and chandeliers. The ceilings were fifteen feet high, the living room big enough to hold a ball, and the master bedroom upstairs was forty feet long and thirty feet wide. The two main rooms were dominated by huge and ancient chandeliers, which our landlord, who owned two Rolls Royces, ran many low-wage enterprises, and professed Christianity, forced us to buy for $500 when we first rented the place.

When the proposition was first put I cabled the *Star* asking for the money and received a reply weeks after we'd paid for them and moved in.

"We have checked and found the *Star* has no official policy about the purchase of antique chandeliers by correspondents," the reply said sternly and apparently seriously. "You will have to pay for them yourself."

After four months packed into two rooms at the Repulse Bay Hotel with the four kids, at a time when accommodation of any sort was virtually unavailable in the crowded colony, we were lucky to get one of the

32

only houses for rent in Hong Kong for the chandelier key money and $2,000 a month, which was about the average price of a good foreign devil apartment.

Although the outside hadn't seen a coat of paint in at least a decade and the creaky big iron gates to the entrance courtyard were constantly falling off their hinges, the place had a little yard, a great rarity in Hong Kong, which looked out over the harbor at the point where the Queen Elizabeth caught fire and burned in 1972. It was being cut to bits by salvage crews at the beginning of our residence, until the big hulk eventually disappeared altogether.

The *Daily Telegraph* correspondent, who lived in a nearby apartment, received a phone call from his London office the day the liner sank asking if the big story was on the way.

"Hang on a sec, old chap, until I look out the window," he told the editor. Then after a pause the reporter's embarrassed voice told London: "By Jove, you're right, you know. The damn thing has sunk."

Chinese squatters lived on the mountain next to our big house and we believed, by the size of our bills, that they tapped our water and electricity supplies. They lived fairly well in their little shanties and were good, quiet neighbors, although one of them, we suspected, was a leftover from the Japanese invasion of World War II because he exercised, with military precision and what looked like a rifle, every morning in front of his cave. Then he dressed in a neat blue business suit and set off for work apparently in a downtown office.

By the time we arrived in Hong Kong in 1973, the traditional Chinese *amah*, or the live-in combination of *amah* and cook-boy, had practically priced themselves off the servants' market. Like many other expatriates, we imported two maids from the Philippines. Our housekeeper was an attractive, intelligent young woman from Mindanao, named Nazaria, who was paid in the beginning HK$450 (U.S.$90) a month. Our "makee learnee" (apprentice) was her cousin Melinda who was paid about half that amount.

In the circumstances Marie didn't cook for almost five years and all meals we ate at home tasted of soya sauce even after we took to hiding the bottle from the two girls. And I wore, I believe, the same set of underwear for months at a time because as soon as I took it off it was washed and put back on top of the pile.

The kids were chauffered in a *pak pai*, an unlicensed, illegal taxi, to the excellent Hong Kong International School by a driver they nicknamed the Assassin in honor of the huge numbers of Chinese he scattered in the narrow streets. They never learned how to make a bed or wash a dish, but they made up for their lack of practical training, we believed, by completely failing in the end to see any difference between people of different races.

The Asian maid business, however, is not entirely the luxury it might seem to hardworking housewives in big homes in parts of the world where high wages have made house servants impossible.

Our girls became part of the already large family and thus they brought Marie their troubles: the brother arrested as a terrorist on Mindanao, the sister who needed money to build a house in Manila, what to wear to Mass, and how to help a Filipino friend who was pregnant. The tears and emotions made the "Missie's" executive and human responsibilities almost as arduous as housework itself.

And there were not only the maids but the old gardener who went with the house but was so old he could hardly walk, let alone work, and the garbage lady who had to be paid to take away the rubbish which she promptly sold to somebody else. Down at

34

the yacht club there was Tamoy, the boat girl, who had to be employed (for U.S.$50 a month) so the sloop wouldn't be robbed or wrecked by whatever boat-boy Triad she had to pay for protection.

Almost all of the eighty or so correspondents in Hong Kong owned a boat or a share in one, mostly diesel-powered junks with their own permanent boat-boy, who did all the work, the sailing and the cooking while the "masters" and their families lounged about on deck with a glass of gin or swam in the clean waters of the outlying islands.

One TV reporter even managed to have his huge floating gin-palace shipped home by his employer at the end of his term. When his office inquired what had to be shipped back with him, he told them: "Only the usual furniture, personal effects, and junk."

But our thirty-foot, fiberglass sloop, built by Hurley in Britain, was a real yacht which we raced with mixed success among the hot local competition and which took us on wonderful, although sometimes adventurous, cruises up the coast of the New Territories, to little islands where the *gweilos* seldom go, and where dirty little fly-blown village restaurants fed us with huge platters of crab and shrimp and fish for about two dollars a head, including a big bottle of beer.

We sailed a few times right to the gloomy, mountainous coast of Mainland China, an easy two- or three-day voyage, until the Communist gunboats turned us back and we fled, our big yellow and black spinnaker billowing among the tattered red sails of the slow, paint-bare fishing junks and their wiry Communist crewmen waving their fists at our sleek little ship.

We did much entertaining in our big home. Every embassy in Hong Kong had its national day to which we were invited and which created a social debt. The

Communist Chinese cadres of the New China News Agency provided many talkative lunches which had to be returned. The political advisers and government China watchers talked most freely over dinner and wine and cognac were cheap in the colony. Other correspondents, visiting from Tokyo or Bangkok, or hit-and-run men from the home office, had to be entertained. A correspondent's job is half diplomacy, a quarter administration, and a quarter real writing work.

In order to do the diplomatic bit with some style, Marie bought a huge rosewood dining room table soon after we arrived in Hong Kong. We watched its progress as it was being made in a tiny, busy factory on the outskirts of Kowloon, marveling at the skill of the carver, who was paid the equivalent of U.S.$120 a month and was therefore comparatively rich, and his twelve-year-old apprentice, who was paid nothing except a few bowls of rice a day.

The table accommodated ten for dinner and it looked magnificent under one of the big old chandeliers. It was Marie's pride and joy until the night it collapsed.

We had decided to repay many of our social debts with one big buffet dinner for about fifty people. The table was loaded with endless varieties of great Cantonese food, cooked in our kitchen by Chinese caterers and kept warm on the table in huge bowls with flames under them.

Our maids had enlisted the aid of four of their friends to help serve the drinks and the conversation was rolling nicely when the Japanese wife of a Canadian diplomat led the way to the table. She had just picked up the first morsel in her chopsticks when the table broke slowly in the middle. The Japanese lady bent gracefully in her kimono, following the food down to the floor. She looked a little surprised and was

36

wondering, perhaps, what a diplomat's wife should do in the unusual circumstances. She solved the problem by squatting on the floor, Japanese style, and continuing to serve herself, as if tables always collapsed miraculously at correspondents' dinners so that Japanese ladies could eat in their traditional way.

But the fires from the heating bowls were burning out of control around her and the food was slithering in all directions and she was pushed gently away by running Chinese cooks who put out the fires, looking highly embarrassed.

The very diplomatic guests moved in other tables from my office and the kitchen and we continued the party which developed, people say, into one of the more lively and certainly most informal of the year's social events.

But the table collapse, which became infamous among Hong Kong's correspondents, continued to cause me trouble for months. The Chinese caterer decided we had lost face and he refused to send me a bill. I wrote him six letters explaining that it wasn't his table and nothing was his fault. But somehow he had lost much face too and he refused to charge anything for this disgrace, even though the amount was considerable.

My pleas for the bill were not based entirely on decency and fairness. I was stuck with a hefty separate bill for liquor and wine, which the *Star*'s accountants in Toronto wouldn't approve without some official indication that it was used for a diplomatic dinner and not for about a year's personal supply or a big booze-up for the boys. I even explained this to the Chinese caterer but still he wouldn't send a bill and in the end he just ignored my letters altogether.

Eventually the bar bill was approved after I sent copies of the correspondence. But the word of the night the Cahill's table collapsed spread quickly through the colony and forever after about half the guests we entertained seemed to surreptitiously press their elbows in testing motions when they sat down to dinner at Marie's magnificent table.

The Foreign Correspondents' Club was our main centre of relaxation. There, on the fifteenth floor of Sutherland House, adjacent to the more prestigious Hong Kong Club, you could order a dozen Australian oysters and a great New York steak for about five dollars with the wine included. Usually you could charge it to expenses and from your table you could watch the cricket match on the green in front of the Bank of China far below.

The view from the men's washroom, over the bustling harbor with its junks down from Canton bucking the tide past the battleships of the U.S. Seventh Fleet at anchor, was even better—the best stand-up view, the club boasted, from any urinals in the world.

But mainly the club was the meeting place for old bush-jacketed friends from the wars, with their stories and gossip and predictions and more importantly their warnings and advice.

"If you're going to the Cambodia border use driver number five at the Oriental Hotel in Bangkok. Name's Mike. Smart old bugger knows where the bandits hit along the road and the refugees with the best stories when you get there . . ."

"I hear you're going to Rhodesia, Jack. I just came over to tell you not to let them rent you a Volkswagen. When you go up to the border, the roads are mined and you've got to follow a big truck right in its tracks so it hits the mines first. A Beetle won't fit. Get a big car. Take care."

"No way you'll get anything out of Bangladesh by phone or wire. Just stand in the lobby of the Intercontinental and ask somebody heading for the airport to pigeon stuff out for you. Take care."

"Take care, old buddy." "Take care, cobber." "Take care, old chap." In a dozen accents it was the casual parting phrase of the correspondent, and it came from the hearts of colleagues who had earned the right to use it.

Old Richard Hughes, the London *Sunday Times* man and model for the character "Old Craw" in John Le Carré's book *The Honorable Schoolboy*, presided with great dignity and a perpetual glass of white wine over this remarkable gathering place. As the dean of the corps of correspondents, we respected him as "Your Eminence" and when we returned from a story he would acknowledge either our success or just our safe return with a slow sign-of-the-Cross blessing.

When I first arrived in Hong Kong, His Eminence, the be-monacled old pro from the wars in China, Japan, Korea, and wherever, greeted me with a blessing and "Welcome, Monsignor."

At a small dinner the night before I left, he patted my shoulder and said, "Goodbye, your Grace. Take care."

It was the most satisfying promotion of my life.

Newspapers should, of course, be absolutely honest with their readers, but the very bylines most of them use on most of their stories from abroad are exercises in deception.

*The Toronto Star*, for instance, now frequently uses the line "*Toronto Star* Special," which seems to indicate that the paper has done something special to obtain the story, when in fact it mostly means "We're sorry but we didn't have anybody there."

*The Globe and Mail*, another Toronto paper, uses its anonymous byline somewhat less deceptively by labelling most non-staff overseas stories "Special to *The Globe and Mail*." This, at least, carries some indication that somebody outside the control of the newspaper produced the story. Papers which cover world news properly, like *The New York Times*, use the phrase accurately by proclaiming that stories by their own writers are "Special to *The New York Times*."

The term "special" was originally applied to the dispatches from the great staff war correspondents of the last century, like William Howard Russell of *The Times* of London, or H. M. Stanley of the New York *Herald*, and their colleagues in the wars in Crimea, the United States, the Sudan, and South Africa.

Now, most of the "special" stories in the Canadian and U.S. press are compiled by editors from American or British wire service stories. Their natural temptation is to shuffle together the more sensational parts of each story, thus sometimes destroying the balance. But many of them come from "stringers," usually freelancers whom neither the foreign editor nor anybody on the newspaper has ever met. Sometimes they are wire service reporters making an extra buck by rewriting their own or their colleague's copy under an assumed name. Sometimes they are people like Paul Vogle, the United Press International (UPI) correspondent, who originally freelanced out of Saigon for years under as many as fourteen different names, creating a few of the world's first female correspondents in the field.

A few of these unknown "special" correspondents, chosen on occasion because of their lack of objection to low payments, are fairly obviously members of the information networks of the United States Central Intelligence Agency (CIA) or perhaps even its Soviet counterpart, the KGB.

In the circumstances a Canadian correspondent

abroad is pestered persistently by prospective "stringers," especially a *Star* correspondent because the *Star* pays maybe $200 a story. The correspondent in the field, however, can usually judge the difference between a genuine professional, a professional who has sold out to one of the intelligence agencies, or a straightforward spook. Sometimes the Canadian embassy staff will warn, with concern, that they believe the stringer they deal with as the official representative of the newspaper is a CIA man and sometimes colleagues from permanent bureaus drop a hint that "our man" seems to have very few visible means of support.

But this situation doesn't appear to worry many evaluators of news in Canada and the U.S. While the intelligence agencies regard the flow and control of information in the world as crucial, many of the big media institutions operate like a bakery with no control over the quality of some of its flour.

It's always hard to be absolutely certain but I have met very few Western staff writers, as opposed to freelancers, abroad who could even be suspected of working for the CIA and, of course, just as few Russian, Chinese, Korean or other Communist bloc journalists who were not obviously and usually overtly working for their governments. This does not mean that Western correspondents have no *unofficial* relationship with the CIA. Almost any of them worth their salt do and so did I. The intelligence agencies and journalists are, after all, in the information business and information is a commodity to be swapped and shared and dealt in. And the CIA man is usually not the covert character of the spy novels, but a fresh-faced U.S. Embassy employee who frankly admits, even advertises, what he does, and can be a good source of information and check against wrong information. The trick is simply to know that you are dealing with a CIA man.

In 1977, toward the end of my term in the Far

East, the CIA was even giving official background briefings to properly accredited correspondents from all countries, on subjects ranging from the capabilities of the Burmese army (considerable) to the political situation in China (confusing), and these were very useful. With the CIA agent subjected to tough questioning from twenty to thirty senior correspondents the message was likely to at least approach the truth.

There is little doubt, however, that some U.S. foreign correspondents depend almost entirely on their embassies, and thus indirectly the CIA, for their information. It is, after all, the natural thing to be attracted to the truth as propounded by one's own countrymen in the embassy offices, at the official briefings, and on the cocktail circuit. It is this information, with its American slant on world affairs, that eventually fills much of Canada's and the Western World's news space.

Personally, I find the smaller embassies—such as the Canadian—more reliable than their U.S. counterparts, depending, of course, on the personalities involved. They usually have access to much CIA and U.S. embassy information anyway and have balanced it through contacts with the others, the British, French, Japanese, Germans, Norwegians, Australians, and whoever, along with often good contacts with the Communist countries. Thus their view of the world is more realistic and unbiased. The ambassador himself is invariably available to the Canadian correspondent and as he doesn't have a great deal of power he doesn't have any special axe to grind.

And Canadian ambassadors are not necessarily colorless, dull diplomats. My favorite was Bill Bauer, for years Canada's representative in Thailand and regarded by his peers as one of the foremost and certainly the frankest of experts on Indo-Chinese affairs. Bauer showed up for work at the embassy on Bangkok's

Silom Road in a pair of old slacks and shirt with no tie and when he took you out to lunch to sort out Indochina's involved problems he did it in a cheap little restaurant on Patpong Road, the infamous brothel and massage parlor area.

But despite this undiplomatic informality, Bauer was a close aquaintance of the King of Thailand, and a frequent guest at the palace where he learned many things.

The first secretary and political advisor in Bauer's embassy until a short while ago was an extremely dapper, good-looking young man, with the unlikely name for a Canadian diplomat of Manfred Von Nostitz. He is the son of a well-known Toronto area horse breeder and I first met him in Can Tho in Vietnam.

In those days Von Nostitz was ensconced in a trailer at the U.S. military airport at Can Tho as one of the brave young diplomats handling the affairs of the peacekeeping International Commission for Control and Supervision. Although he was constantly traveling, often in helicopters attacked by ground fire, between the representatives of the South Vietnamese and the Viet Cong, he did it in a suit that looked as if it had just come from Ottawa's best tailor, and there was always a tennis racquet on his cot where we sat to wonder about the realities of the American "peace with honor."

A joint briefing by Bauer and Von Nostitz in Bangkok was always a journalistic joy and their advice, political and personal, invariably right on.

"For Christ's sake," Von Nostitz would warn at the end of his political briefing. "Keep away from the girls on Patpong Road. They've got a dose now that defies all the penicillin in the world."

43

CHAPTER 3

# The night the brothel burned

There are some great hotels in Asia. The old Repulse
Bay Hotel in Hong Kong is one of them, with its huge
rooms and antique furniture, its running room boys,
and the marks of Japanese bullets from the World War
II invasion still on some of the thick cement walls.

While we were looking for a permanent home and
office on the island, my family and I lived for four
months at the Repulse Bay. We had two rooms,
paneled in rich wood, with ceilings about fifteen feet
high. We overlooked the long, pure white beach, with
its constant crowd of ice cream and hot dog devouring
Hong Kong Chinese, who seemed desperate, for some
reason I have never understood, to tan themselves.

Beyond the beach the fleets of local fishing junks
spread their nets and the old, unpainted junks, down
from Canton or other parts of the Communist
mainland, sometimes passed by. Their crews strained
at long oars when the wind was still but usually their
patched and faded red sails billowed in a breeze.

The balcony of the Repulse Bay is one of the
world's best places to eat and the setting among the

44

world's most exotic. But even the best French food becomes a bit boring after a few months so that we came to prefer the simpler meals of the coffee shop or the steaks barbecued on the hotel's broad lawns in the balmy evenings.

Raffles in Singapore, once the rambling, white second home of the British planters, is a little run-down now, with an occasional cockroach and furniture that is old without being antique. It is still a nice place to stay if you can manage to ignore the lines of tourists who gawk at you, clutching their complimentary Singapore Slings, as you dine in the magnificent dusk of the open-air Palm Court, with its starched linen and candelabra, green lawn and waving palms.

My favorite is the old section of the Oriental Hotel in Bangkok, where the two-storey rooms—comfortable living area below and bedroom above—overlook the muddy river. One can watch a stream of sampans, loaded with fruit and flowers, dead pigs and people; the long, narrow, motorized ferries, low in the water with workers and tourists; and at night the twinkling lights and cooking fires of the adventurous city.

The Taj Mahal in Bombay is magnificently ornate and efficient, its foyer constantly crowded with the rich of the poor land and their beautiful ladies in flowing saris. The new Sheraton in the same city is perhaps even more luxurious in a more modern way. You can see, from the plush comfort of your suite, hordes of ordinary Indians in a shanty town almost directly below, sleeping in the heat under slanting scraps of galvanized iron, making their homes in packing cases, gathering in big families around a cooking fire with small bowls of rice, their meal for the day. As you sip your Scotch you can see the women carrying on their heads the pitchers of water from some dirty well and you can ponder the plight of these people, who live on less in a year than you have to pay for a night at the hotel.

Hotels like these help the foreign correspondent.

45

In the back of his mind he knows he can usually escape to one of them, often to dine in considerable style, in some places with a bottle of reasonable wine, while he contemplates what he will write about those real people in that other world he works in. This ability to escape gives him a troubled conscience sometimes. But in a strange way the blatant contrast can also encourage his sympathies and enforce his objectivity. At least he realizes that he is a very fortunate fellow indeed.

However, not all hotels in Asia are oases of riches and luxury in a desert of poverty and underprivilege. The Majestic Hotel, for instance, in Can Tho in the Mekong Delta of Vietnam, is different.

Photographer Boris Spremo and I checked into the Majestic one evening in 1973, partly because we had been told it was to become the headquarters for the Canadian forces assigned to the ICCS peacekeeping force in that area, and partly because it seemed to be the only hotel in town.

We were tired. We had tried to sleep the previous night in an abandoned barracks at Saigon's Tan Son Nhut airport. This was because the Vietnamese, for some reason, would not let us near the area of the airport where the Canadian peacekeeping forces were setting up their main headquarters. They had arrested a Canadian photographer and thrown him in jail. We were smuggled into the airport on the floor of an ICCS car and hid in the abandoned barracks so that we could catch the chopper to Can Tho in the morning.

The barracks was full of mosquitoes and the few thrown-away mattresses in it were full of fleas so we didn't sleep except for a few minutes on the flight. We were told when we landed that the chopper had run through a few rounds of ground fire as we slept.

At the Can Tho air base we had picked up a jeep with a Vietnamese driver who spoke fairly good English and we spent most of the day at another airport on the outskirts of the town trying to interview a group of about a hundred female Viet Cong soldiers. The women were squatting glumly in their black pyjama suits under conical hats on the hot tarmac, waiting to be flown to North Vietnam in the first stage of a prisoner exchange.

At first the American officers wouldn't let us near them but after hours of negotiation they allowed us to interview a Canadian captain who was in charge of policing the exchange and he agreed to turn his back while we talked to the women through the driver-interpreter, providing Spremo took no pictures.

All the women would do was snarl at us. Some of them spat. None of them would say a word. But Spremo managed to shoot a few pictures from the hip, the first Western pictures of the prisoner exchange and the first in many years of Viet Cong women soldiers.

When we asked the driver what they had said when he approached them he look embarrassed and said it wouldn't exactly translate. But when we asked him to try anyway, he told us, "They said I was a running dog of the Yankee imperialist bastards. You were the shit of the earth and we should all fuck off.

"I've never met any Viet Cong women before," he said with a note of distress in his voice. "They are not very nice."

The driver, who chewed constantly on a dead grasshopper, as many Mekong Delta men do for some narcotic reason, eventually drove us between the open sewers that line the highway to the town. On its outskirts, not far from the American base, he pointed to a ramshackle shack bearing a big sign in English proclaiming "The Happy Fuck."

"Number one bar that," he said, chewing on his grasshopper. "Hell of a good place. Not very pricey."

When we got to the Majestic Hotel, a four- or five-storey building across the dusty main road from the Mekong River, he described it similarly and, we should have realized, ominously. "Number one place," he said. "Not very pricey. Lots of fun place."

When Spremo and I checked in we were given the numbers of rooms on the second floor, but no keys. And when I began to open the door to my room a shrill voice shouted something in Vietnamese which sounded similar to the remarks of the Viet Cong women at the airport.

While I was contemplating this situation, Spremo emerged from his room across the corridor clutching his nose and looking strangely pale.

"I try to go to the bathroom," he said in the thick Yugoslav accent he hasn't lost in two decades in Canada. "I open the door and the smell knocks me over. So I slam the smell in so it can't get out. I think there is something dead in the bathroom. Do you have a bathroom?"

"I don't know yet," I told him. "There's somebody in my room."

We went to the clerk on the first floor who had booked us in and told him there was something dead in Boris' bathroom and somebody alive in my room and he shrugged and told us to wait a while and he'd fix it up. Then after about five minutes he told us to go back to our rooms. Now mine was empty except for two cockroaches as big as frogs in the corner. They were too big to stomp on because of the mess they would have made. And there was a rat running round inside the glass lampshade. It made the already dim light come in oddly varying intensities as it moved around the bulb.

There was a small, low bed in the room with a dirty cover and that was all, except for a door with peeling paint leading to a bathroom. I opened it with great care. There was a hole in the bare and filthy cement floor for a toilet and a rusty pipe in a corner with a shower attachment.

A woman knocked at the room door while I was surveying the bathroom and asked if I wanted her to stay. She was very fat and she didn't seem to have any teeth and she got quite upset when I told her to go away. Spremo was upset too when he knocked and he looked even paler than before.

"I open the door again just a little bit," he said. "And the stench you wouldn't believe. There is something dead in there, maybe some*body*. I not open the door again. Do you have a bathroom?"

Boris used the bathroom and emerged looking a little better. "You cheated," he accused me. "You took the room with the good bathroom."

"Boris," I said, "I have become convinced that, in general, this is not one of the better hotels." I showed him the rat in the lampshade.

The food wasn't very good either in the restaurant on the ground floor, mainly rice with a shrimp or two in it, and while we were eating the kitchen exploded and the building caught fire. Jets of fire spurted suddenly toward our table, as if from a flame thrower. The kitchen was a yelling mess of brown men and burning fat. We ran into the street.

Spremo can be an excitable fellow especially if anything occurs that might stop him doing his job, and the first thing he thought of, maybe the only thing, was his precious collection of cameras hidden under the bed in his room.

He ran through the hotel's main entrance up the staircase and although it was the opposite of common sense I followed him. The stairs were on fire and we were scorched a bit as we ran down them, clutching cameras, typewriter, and notebooks.

Then we stood in the street and watched the arrival of a fire brigade consisting of scores of shrilly vocal men towing galvanized tanks of water on hand carts.

There is something funny about a burning brothel. Maybe there shouldn't be, but there is. It is not the déshabille of the emerging clientele, but the expressions on their faces. This is a strange mixture of shock and shame, combined with false attempts at casual unconcern and complete detachment, probably unseen on the human face except in these circumstances. There is also no gallantry in a burning brothel. The men, all of them Vietnamese or Chinese, because the Majestic was obviously an institution for wealthier locals, charged first down the burning stairs, pulling up pants and pushing the girls aside so that the towels some of them had wrapped around their bodies were ripped away and they were running around with only two hands and three or four places to put them.

Despite their primitive equipment, the yelling fire brigade managed somehow to confine the fire to the restaurant and staircase and part of the first floor of the hotel and put it out after an hour or so, so Spremo and I were able to return to our rooms to sleep. But Boris never did open his bathroom door again. And I tried not to disturb the rat and the cockroaches. Twice during the night I managed to be polite in rejecting disheveled ladies who seemed to be going for fire sale prices.

There are many great hotels in Asia and the image of the foreign correspondent living the luxurious life, even covering the wars from the comfort of his suite, is sometimes justified. But the Majestic in Can Tho is not one of these hotels. And unfortunately on some jobs there are just as many Majestics as there are Taj Mahals.

In the long run, to save expenses, I learned to dispense with Spremo and his photographer colleagues and to take my own pictures, which was a mistake. It is risky to travel alone anywhere in the world. In the troubled areas where the stories are it is stupid. It is also impossible to observe an occurrence properly through the lens of a Nikon. You either focus on one point and miss the overall picture or you stand back and observe a situation objectively and fully and miss the picture on film.

In a war situation the photographer has to take many more risks than the writer. He has to walk those extra ten yards or so into the minefield to get the best angle, or stand upright in the ditch to get his shot. Those extra ten yards make the difference and they take guts. To do his work the photographer has to stay and face the problem while the writer is running away from artillery shells or a mob. The cameramen, TV and still, are the journalistic heroes of the wars.

But throughout the period of covering the Canadian ICCS corps in Vietnam, the ebullient, excitable, handsome Spremo, winner of more than 150 awards and one of the world's best hard news photographers, was with me, raring to get where the action was, hustling to get back to Saigon to wire his pictures through the Associated Press (AP) or UPI wire services, fretting at my insistence that I had to talk to people sometimes, or go somewhere where there would be no picture. He threw some of the best parties in Saigon for his photographer friends—except for the one time he bought his Scotch on the black market and served his guests with pure urine.

Shortly before the experience at the Majestic we had flown up to Hue, the ancient spiritual capital of Vietnam, along with John Walker, of Southam News Service, to cover the Canadians setting up their headquarters for peacekeeping in the northern areas. They were establishing themselves in an old hotel on the banks of the Perfume River. Two officers who had been sent to operate an outpost in the bombed out city of Quang Tri, on the border between North and South

Vietnam, had been unable to reach the city. They had met with heavy artillery fire on the way and been forced to turn back.

Walker, Spremo, and I, and an NBC TV crew from Chicago, who were in the area ahead of us, decided, over a huge meal of crab and beer at the Canadian headquarters, that it would be a good story if we went in where the peacekeepers didn't dare go. In so doing, we thought, we could illustrate the difficulties of peacekeeping in a war that wasn't over, although everybody in North America appeared to have swallowed the Kissinger-Nixon line that there was not only peace in Vietnam but also honor.

The NBC men made a deal. They had a letter of introduction to a South Vietnamese general at a headquarters near Quang Tri, who might allow us into the city. We had a Canadian flag which might be recognized as a symbol of neutrality and stop somebody shooting at us. We'd be the NBC crew as far as the general was concerned. They'd be Canadians if any shooting started.

We rented two white-painted jeeps and their drivers, bargaining expensively for them in advance and depleting the cash supply of our Canadian group to almost nothing. But the drivers assured us the banks would be open and would take traveler's cheques on our return to Hue, so we could then purchase Air Vietnam tickets to get back to Saigon to file our stories.

We set out in a two-jeep convoy, with the Canadian flag flying from our leading vehicle, across the bombed-down and patched-together bridges on the road to Quang Tri, about sixty miles away. In the little villages of huts made from ammunition crates and shell casings, the main economic activity seemed to be coffin making, because every village had three or four coffin shops.

Soldiers stopped us at checkpoints along the way, wondered about the white and red maple leaf flag and let us through after we explained we were *bo chi* (journalists) from a neutral, peacekeeping country. Some of them seemed to know where Canada was, but they thought it was a part of the U.S. anyway and we had to explain the peace treaty and the role of the ICCS to them.

The village where the general had his headquarters was off the main highway not far from Quang Tri, and the NBC letter of introduction worked. The general gave us a note instructing his men in the city to look after us. But he also warned us not to go.

A shell exploded in a deep ditch, about a hundred yards behind our jeeps, as we turned onto the main highway again, sending a column of water high in the air, and a heavy artillery barrage hit along the roadside as we appraoched the city.

Quang Tri, once the home of over 60,000 people, is in fact not a city. It is a horrible mess of rubble, a collection of huge pockmarks from the bombs of B-52s. It looked like the surface of the moon, with nothing standing higher than a few feet except one little bombed-out building. The only inhabitants were four Vietnamese soldiers and a captain in faded battledress and an obvious state of fatigue in this one predominant pile of rubble which used to be the city's hospital.

We could see a South Vietnamese flag flying at the edge of where the city had been and beyond that, across the river, a Viet Cong flag. And to the east, half a mile away, the artillery barrage was hitting, about a shell a minute, mostly in approximately the same place, sending up columns of black smoke and making much noise.

Spremo wanted a picture of the two flags with the artillery barrage in the background. So did the NBC crew. But the Vietnamese captain said we couldn't go closer because the whole area was mined and two of his men had been killed the previous day. But it was too much for the NBC crew. They knew what their zoom

53

lens could do with the artillery barrage—even though it was so far away—and the two flags in the background while the correspondent did his stand up stuff. They'd get maybe thirty seconds of air time despite the fact that Vietnam was not making the tube at home at all any more.

And Spremo knew what his long-distance lenses could do, providing he got the right angle.

So eventually the captain, who wore a very tired smile, said we could go as long as we walked exactly in the footsteps of a soldier he would send to lead the way through the minefield. And he stressed that he meant that exactly, by making us practice in the safe dirt near his rubble headquarters, stepping single file in the footsteps of the man in front.

It occurred to me during the practice that there was no need for me to go at all because I could see all that was happening perfectly well for my purposes from where I was. In fact, it seemed eminently commonsensical not to go.

"Hey Boris," I said casually. "There's really no need for John and I to go. We can see it all from here."

Spremo didn't say anything. Neither did Walker nor the NBC crew, nor the Vietnamese captain. There was just a silence. So I said, "OK, I'm coming," and we went, picking our way painstakingly in the short footsteps of the little soldier, until Spremo, looking through the lens of his Nikon at the smoke from the artillery barrage, began to wander away off course, and I had to run after him, swearing at him, to pull him back into the line.

We could see the Viet Cong soldiers in their black battledress on the other side of the river and we waved to them, but they just stared back with puzzled expressions. The artillery barrage intensified cooperatively just as the NBC man was doing his thing in front of the camera and the sound man muttered gleefully, "Good bang bangs, great bang bangs." Spremo got some good pictures.

Perhaps it was because most of us were looking at it through long-distance lenses, but the barrage seemed to be coming closer so we picked our way more hurriedly back through the minefield to the jeeps. It was noon now and the plane to Saigon, the only place from where we could wire the film and file our stories, left Hue at 2:30 P.M. It was already midnight in Toronto, only six hours before the morning deadline. But lots of time, really, even though we had to stop at the bank in Hue to get some money to pay our fares.

The NBC crew sped away and we didn't see them again. They were to stay in Hue to do some more stories. They could ship their film on the plane and have it picked up in Saigon. The TV crews always had good logistical backups, but newspaper people rarely do, except perhaps those from *The New York Times* and one or two other major newspapers with staffs in Saigon. We had to carry our own stuff.

We were tired by now. Walking across minefields is an emotional drain. The noise of the artillery barrage had been wearying, even though it never came really close to us. And as we passed through one of the little coffin villages the front wheels of the jeep began to wobble violently. The driver pulled to the side of the road looking sheepish.

Spremo doesn't like this sort of thing to happen when he has undeveloped film of consequence in his camera. He becomes excited. He jumped from the jeep and began kicking the wheels and ordering the driver to drive on anyway. The driver produced a big hammer from the back of the jeep and for a while I thought he was going to hit Spremo with it. But instead he hit the jeep wheels hard and many times, then finally agreed we should drive slowly on. We had wasted about half an hour.

When we got to the bank at Hue on the wobbly wheels it was after 1:30 P.M. and the bank was closed until 3 P.M. for a siesta period the driver had forgotten to warn us about. This made Spremo angry again but he calmed down when I said we'd ask the Canadian ICCS team, in the headquarters across the river, to lend us the money for our air fares.

On the way, halfway across the bridge, the jeep finally gave up altogether. One of the wheels fell off. Spremo tried to put it back on, covering his bush jacket with grease in the process, but it didn't work and the driver promised he'd find another jeep somewhere. In the meantime we ran about a mile in the hundred-degree heat to the ICCS headquarters.

When we had stopped puffing and sweating enough to make sense of ourselves, the captain in charge said fine, he'd lend us the money, but all of the cash in the post's possession was, for some reason he never explained, in a car on the way to the airport. If we could find the car, he said, we should tell the sergeant it was OK to take what we needed as long as we gave him a receipt.

In the meantime our driver had turned up at the headquarters in a new jeep, but its wheels too began to wobble almost uncontrollably on the way to the airport. And we never found the ICCS car with the money.

The Air Vietnam Boeing 707 was already boarding when we arrived and the tumbledown terminal was packed with a babbling horde, clutching string bags and baskets and clamoring for the few spare seats still apparently available.

Spremo became excited again. He spoke in English to the pretty girl in a yellow *ao dai* who was selling the tickets, stating what must have been obvious —he had about six cameras hanging from his neck— that he was a photographer who had to get to Saigon in

56

a hurry and that we would all pay our fares by cheque now or by cash after we got to Saigon. She smiled at him.

He tried it again in primitive French, in a somewhat higher pitch, and the girl began to look puzzled. Then he began shouting at her in Yugoslavian, pounding the ticket counter. She began to look distressed.

There was one other European in the terminal who looked as if he might be a journalist so I introduced myself. He was a nice young man from the Knight newspapers in the States and he emptied his wallet of piastres so that we were able to scrape up just enough between us all to buy our tickets.

Walker and I wrote our stories during the two-hour flight and we arrived at Tan Son Nhut airport with several hours to spare before my morning Toronto deadline. But the long drive to downtown Saigon in the afternoon rush hour is never easy and this time it was worse than usual. The streets were packed with screaming Hondas, carrying anything from two to five people. Bullock carts blocked several intersections and army trucks crawled ahead of us. A crooked cop (assuming there were any who weren't crooked) pulled us aside near the big Buddhist temple and bargained with the driver for more than half an hour before he was able to elicit enough bribe money to allow us to proceed.

There was only one way to file a story quickly out of Saigon in those days. The wire services, especially Reuters which I always used, did their best, but there was invariably a pile of stories in their baskets at this time of day and one was expected to ask for priority over colleagues only in highly exceptional circumstances. The only quick way was through a single telephone booth in an old building kitty-corner from the Caravelle Hotel on Tu Do Street. From here, after bribing the clerk in charge of phone calls, you could get a direct line to Oakland, California, and be switched through to Canada.

You have to close the door to this tiny phone booth to deaden the noise of the Hondas outside. Then no air gets in and it is the hottest place on earth. There is nowhere to put your notes as you dictate a story so the combination of oozing sweat from your hands and big drips from your face makes your notes soggy and unreadable. I have seen reporters come from this phone booth, remove their bush jackets, and wring them out like wet towels. And this particular day was a hot one. What sweat I had left after the mile run in Hue poured out onto my notes.

When I got through to the foreign desk in Toronto, a young editor who had just come on shift was grumpy.

"I wish you'd learn to file earlier, Jack," he said. "It's only an hour before deadline. It's a hell of a busy day. And I had a tough time getting to work in the traffic this morning."

I was too tired and sweaty to argue.

"Will you just get me a copytaker?" I said.

# CHAPTER 4

# If you don't like the war, switch the damn thing off!

When Henry Kissinger, the U.S. presidential adviser, won a Nobel Peace Prize for bringing a settlement to Vietnam, the American people, and others throughout the Western world, tended to take the award seriously.

There was a widespread belief abroad that the hyperactive and unusual diplomat had indeed organized something remarkable in his long negotiations with North Vietnamese emissary Le Duc Tho in Paris throughout 1972, and at the final peace talks in Paris in January, 1973. People wanted to believe that Kissinger had put an end to the war that had killed more than a million men, including over 56,000 Americans, and had created a crisis of conscience for almost twelve years in the United States.

In particular, the men in the executive offices of the TV networks in New York believed the claims by Kissinger and President Richard Nixon that they had at last achieved "peace with honor" in Vietnam. This was partly because, like most other good Americans, they desperately wanted to believe it, partly because the war coverage was expensive, and also because, with the final withdrawal of American troops in 1973, stories from the area would be without American content and therefore without much news value.

There's no story, someone said, in gooks killing gooks.

In Vietnam, though, the war went on. About 10,000 Vietnamese continued to die every month in the slaughter. Families still wept at the big cemetery at Bien Hua outside Saigon where the dead soldiers were buried. In the village of An My, twenty-five miles north of Saigon, Mrs. Phan Thi-Xinh, an elderly widow, woke up in the early hours of the morning of January 28, 1973, the official date of the ceasefire, to find eight dead soldiers in the patch of banana trees behind her home. Later that day her little stone house was destroyed in an artillery attack. She didn't believe me when I told her the Americans said the war was over.

In Ottawa, Canadian External Affairs Minister Mitchell Sharp was almost as sceptical as Mrs. Xinh so he was startled when he received a phone call from U.S. Secretary of State William Rogers announcing, just before the peace pact was concluded, that Canada had been nominated to the four-member International Commission of Control and Supervision (ICCS) to police the peace.

Neither Sharp, nor Prime Minister Pierre Trudeau, nor any other Canadian official, had ever been consulted about possible Canadian participation in the peacekeeping force and Sharp, a normally calm, phlegmatic man, gasped at the presumption of his American counterpart and at the blatant intrusion into Canadian affairs.

But Rogers persisted. Negotiations in Paris were delicate, he said. If Canada pulled out it would ruin the agreement. Surely Canada wouldn't want to do anything to ruin the chances of peace in Vietnam.

"We were put in a terrible spot," Sharp told me later, after he'd ended a distinguished political career. "We were, of course, very interested in peace in Vietnam, but it was our opinion that the terms of the treaty were unrealistic and that there was, in fact, no peace in Vietnam. We were in effect being committed by the Americans to send Canadian troops into a situation in which many of them could be killed."

A few days later, on a Sunday morning, a group of eight Canadian external affairs officials sat at the long table in the "operations room" in the East Block of Ottawa's Parliament Buildings and played a deadly serious game.

Some of them pretended they were Hungarians while others played the roles of Poles or Indonesians, the other three nationalities which were "invited" to participate, along with Canada, in the proposed peacekeeping force. All of them, from time to time, switched back to playing the part of Canadians in the force, an easy role because most of them had had long, often frustrating, personal experience in Southeast Asia with the ineffective Internal Control Commission (ICC) formed under the Geneva agreement of 1954 to report on outbreaks of hostilities in Indo-China. Poland and India were the other ICC members.

These eight men, joined at times by other top external affairs and defence department officials, argued and pleaded and tried out all of their diplomatic tricks for more than sixteen hours without a break, until about three the following morning, when they were all exhausted.

They reached the basic conclusion that the peacekeeping operation proposed by Kissinger at the Paris peace talks, and pushed on Canada by Secretary of State Rogers, would not work.

Worse, these weary men decided, Canada could be trapped as a scapegoat, blamed for the naivete of Kissinger and Nixon, if it participated in a peacekeeping operation which was certain to fail. At the same time, however, they drew up a rigid set of rules, based on Canada's eighteen years of experience in Vietnam with the ICC, which might make peacekeeping practicable, if rigidly applied.

Sharp then unleashed a flurry of diplomatic activity around the world that confirmed the gloomy judgement of the eight men in the "operations room." Nick Etheridge, Canada's man in Hanoi, tried to consult with the North Vietnamese government but was able to contact only some minor officials. Subsequently David Jackson, Canada's senior representative in Saigon flew into Hanoi on an ICC aircraft and received assurance from high officials in the foreign ministry that Canada would be acceptable as one of the peacekeeping participants. But when he mentioned Canada's conditions he was told: "Let's have peace first, then we can discuss details."

He was also told that North Vietnam envisaged a peacekeeping force of about 250 men compared with the 1,500 contemplated by the Americans.

John Halstead, then assistant under-secretary of state for external affairs, flew to Warsaw and Budapest for talks with the Poles and Hungarians. The Poles indicated they understood Canada's concerns in light of their common experience as members of the ICC, but the Hungarians suggested it should be an honor to serve on such a commission and said they didn't want to get bogged down with details. And from Indonesia, the other nonCommunist member, Ambassador Tom Delworth, an old Indochina hand, reported that there would be many complexities.

Still, Sharp was stuck with the American warning that if Canada rejected a role in the force there might be no peace treaty. He agreed that Canada would participate for sixty days providing the conditions laid down by the eight men in the "operations room" game were met. "I don't know if the Americans tried to negotiate the conditions or not," Sharp said later. "But we didn't get most of them."

Frustrated and disgusted, bitterly opposed by many of his own officials, a full forty-five percent of whom had cut their diplomatic teeth in Southeast Asia, Sharp pushed approval for participation through Parliament. And because the key condition—that a "continuing political authority" like the United Nations Security Council, would assume responsibility for the peace settlement and receive reports from the commission or any of its members—was not achieved, he proclaimed a unilateral "open mouth policy." This meant that Canada would say what it liked, through the press or any vehicle available, and thus, in effect, report directly to the free world.

The "open mouth" policy made coverage of the ICCS activities in Vietnam a ball. Sharp appointed Michel Gauvin, the Canadian ambassador to Greece, to take charge of the peacekeeping operation from Saigon. He talked his head off to the press, to the Americans, to the North Vietnamese, and the Viet Cong, and he told everybody else what he had told the others and what they had told him. Within his first week in Saigon he was nicknamed "Open Mouth" Gauvin.

The *Star's* Mark Gayn wrote: "If Michel Gauvin didn't exist we would have had to invent him for the peacekeeper's job in South Vietnam. Indeed, it is difficult to think of another person who could have done as well in the face of such handicaps of human hostility, twisted politics and unkind nature."

Gleefully, Gauvin blasted off in an oddly undiplomatic way at the Poles, the Hungarians, the Americans, or anybody else whenever he felt the urge, creating embarrassment almost everywhere and huge amounts of respect and gratitude amongst the members of the small press corps covering the ICCS activities.

And Gauvin was only the leader of the "open mouths." Even corporals among Canada's 290-man peace force held forth to the press or anybody who wanted to listen to their views. They discussed world affairs, the progress of the alleged peace, the stupidities of their colleagues from the Communist countries, their disgust with American bureaucracy, and anything else they wanted to say as citizens of a free country that believed in free speech—even for unfortunates in the Army.

I was shuttling between Saigon and Ottawa at this stage of the story and in Ottawa the press spokesman for the department of external affairs, Dick Gorham, another old Southeast Asia hand, was out-blabbing even the great Open Mouth Gauvin. At one background briefing in the Parliament buildings he criticized us for not asking the right questions. Then he told us that the right questions to ask concerned Canadian-American relations. "And if you want to know the answers," he added, "I just happen to have some highly confidential documents I'll leave on the desk here in case anybody wants to take a surreptitious peek on the way out."

In Vietnam, because of the American commitment of Canada to the cause, Canadian servicemen and diplomats were shot at, their helicopters were the targets of heat-seeking SAM missiles, their peacekeeping outposts umbrella'd by artillery barrages, and the roads they traveled heavily mined. Fortunately only one Canadian was killed, when a SAM hit a helicopter, and two held as captives by the Viet Cong, as alleged U.S. spies, before Sharp and the Canadian government pulled out the "peacekeepers" after a sixty-day extension of the original sixty-day term.

In the circumstances, early in 1973, there was some newspaper space and airtime for the war in Canada, but very little anywhere else in the world. The Canadian interest also evaporated rapidly as soon as the "peacekeepers" were called home. The

American people continued to heave their great sigh of relief that the war was over and the TV executives in New York continued to do nothing to convince them otherwise. The foreign correspondents drank or grumbled their frustrations away in the clubs of Hong Kong, Bangkok, and Tokyo. And the Vietnamese continued to destroy each other in enormous ugly numbers.

Peter Hively, the Asian bureau chief for the American Broadcasting Company, came to our home in Hong Kong for dinner one evening in mid 1973 and announced, with a dazed look on his face, that his office had ordered him to go to Saigon to close down the network's bureau there.

"But the war's not over," I said. "Did you tell them the war isn't over?"

"I told them maybe a dozen times," Hively said. "But they said we have peace with honor in Vietnam and there's nothing happening there. They said Kissinger says the war is over. Nixon says the war is over. So the war's over. And when I insisted the war wasn't over they treated me as if I was some sort of nut. They just wouldn't believe me."

In the end, Hively said, he thought the only way he could convince the bureaucrats in the head office that the war still waged was to insist on combat pay, a small supplement paid to some U.S. correspondents in war zones, before he'd go to Saigon to close the bureau. But even that didn't work.

"They told me that was OK," he said. "They said I could have combat pay to go to Vietnam to close the bureau because the war was over.

"They just don't want to believe us. They don't like the war so they've switched the damn thing off," he said.

Hively's aircraft had to swerve to avoid a few artillery fights before it landed in Saigon, but he closed the bureau and he collected his combat pay.

Through 1973, 1974, up to the early spring of 1975, the world's great apathy towards the wars in Indo-China continued unabated. The correspondents were called home or they found their stories elsewhere, watching, mostly from Hong Kong or Tokyo, the beginning of the demise of Chairman Mao Tse-tung in China, the struggle of Japan to continue the economic miracle, and the increasing megalomania of India's prime minister, Indira Gandhi.

Among the eighty or so correspondents based in Hong Kong, only a few, mostly magazine writers, were allowed to take any direct interest in the events in Vietnam and they were on long-term projects with vague, unurgent deadlines.

Tony Paul, the huge, able Australian roving editor for *Reader's Digest*, occasionally brought firsthand news of the war back to the rest of us at the Foreign Correspondents' Club and we could understand from the wires the frustrations of the few correspondents still in Saigon. But still there was no interest at home.

Paul's editors had sensibly asked him to research and write a piece for the U.S. editions entitled "Can South Vietnam Survive the Peace?" But the events caught up with the idea, and eventually with Paul himself, before the article could be published.

Paul flew to Saigon in November, 1974, to interview U.S. Ambassador Graham Martin, who told him: "About ten years from now, South Vietnam will be a rich little capitalist country with a minor problem of Communist terrorism in its remoter border provinces —really nothing more than banditry, the sort of problem that many other Asian nations have to contend with."

Then he had trouble arranging his most important interview—until he was suddenly advised in Hong Kong that the president, Nguyen Van Thieu, would receive him at his palace in Saigon on Saturday, March 8, 1975.

Uncomfortable in an unaccustomed business suit and itching in the heat, Paul was met by the shrewd, tough, corrupt president on the patio of the palace. It was the last interview given by Thieu as president of the Republic of South Vietnam.

Thieu said he was deeply worried about the growing reluctance of the U.S. Congress to grant more aid for his country, but nevertheless he was highly optimistic about economic developments at home. The rice crop had never been better, he said. American and Canadian companies appeared to have discovered major offshore oil deposits likely to be earning millions of dollars by 1979. Capital would be flowing into the country as soon as businessmen realized the advantages of South Vietnam's cheap labor and her new laws encouraging foreign investors.

Paul asked him why he had granted the interview at this particular time.

"Oh," said Thieu casually, "I've just finished a reorganization of the civil service and I've got some spare time on my hands."

At almost the exact moment that Thieu was expressing his languorous optimism on his palace patio a small group of Communist signalers were checking surreptitiously into the Anh Dao Hotel in Ban Me Thout, 300 miles away in South Vietnam's Central Highlands. They set up their smuggled radios on the top floors of the old hotel and at first light the next day, acting as spotters, they began to direct a massive artillery barrage against the headquarters compound and the tank and artillery bases of the town's defenders, the 23rd Division of the Army of the Republic of Vietnam (ARVN).

The men on the hotel roof also signalled the start of the end of the war. Within two days Ban Me Thout had fallen, threatening the security of the two larger Central Highlands towns of Pleiku and Kontum. Within a week Thieu had ordered the disastrous retreat from all of the highlands. Just fifty-three days after Thieu's optimistic interview on the palace patio, the North Vietnamese tanks rolled across the palace lawns and men from the jungles, wearing pith helmets, were patrolling the palace balconies, gaping at the unknown wonders of a city as they strolled Tu Do Street. They complained to the staff of the Caravelle Hotel that when they put their rice for washing in the toilet bowls, it disappeared down the drains of the "rice washing machines."

When the Central Highlands fell in mid-March of 1975, and Saigon thus seemed to be vaguely threatened, the TV executives in New York switched the war on again. The newspaper editors began to see on the screen what they hadn't wanted to believe was happening. Rooms in the correspondents' hotels, the Caravelle and the Continental Palace, opposite each other in Saigon's main city square, suddenly became scarce again. Rumuntcho's restaurant, where most of us ate most of the time, had to use its upstairs room to look after the overflow.

These were good days for a correspondent in Saigon. There were stories and excitement without much danger. Old friends arrived almost daily from all parts of the world. The food was good at Rumuntcho's, especially the cheese soufflé, and the house wine served in wooden jugs was cheap, plentiful, and respectable. Or you could dine with more class on the French cuisine at the Guilliaume Tell, sit over an endless variety of Vietnamese crab dishes at the big restaurant on the riverfront, overlooking the old Saigon Yacht Club, or try, for a change, the Chinese restaurants of Cholon. During the day, if you had time, you could swim or play tennis with the rich establishment at the exclusive *Cercle Sportif*.

The same old drivers we had used in the days of the "real" war, with the same old rattletrap cars, greeted us like old friends and fought for our services, offering everything from cheaper, newer, better girls to cheaper and quicker civil servants in charge of the issuance of exit visas and curfew passes.

With the Americans gone there was a glut of girls. Many of them were semi-amateurs and still beautiful, but the ravages of war were obvious in the painted faces and sloppy bodies of the battered professionals in the dark bars along Tu Do Street. They were also desperate. They rattled embarrassingly on the bar windows as you passed, trying to encourage you inside with smiles so false and gestures so crude they'd discourage, surely, even the randiest of rapists.

But the hostesses at the rooftop bar of the Miramar Hotel were mostly new or attractive still in their colorful *ao dais* and, as ever, they could be charged as room service on the hotel bill if you were staying there.

One Scandinavian TV correspondent, who lived with his crew at the Miramar, fell seriously and genuinely in love with a beautiful, blond secretary at one of the Scandinavian embassies, but was unable to impress her even after weeks of intense and ardent effort. Finally, on his birthday, she agreed to be entertained briefly, for a drink and a chat, in his hotel room.

But the correspondent's crew had also decided to give him a birthday present—three girls from the rooftop bar.

When he entered his room with the innocent secretary on his arm, they were met by a roomful of naked ladies shouting, as instructed by the crew: "Happy Birthday! Have a fuck!"

The Scandinavian was very gloomy about his broken romance for about a week afterward, but he recovered, and eventually even made friends again with his crew.

The city was normal and the people went about their business as usual. Con Cua (The Crab)—the beggar boy with a paralysed spine—continued to crawl along Tu Do Street on all fours and the noseless leper plied his constant trade in front of the Catholic Cathedral. The widows of the war begged as usual in the restaurants and the "homeless," using rented, skinny, starving kids, hustled agressively in the streets for a few coins. The ex-soldiers with no legs thumped the pavements with their arms and stumps to attract attention.

The enormous talents of Ti Ti, the jasmine girl, had been honed to perfection by now. Ti Ti (Vietnamese for littlest one) was about six years old and knee-high to a 105-millimeter howitzer shell. If you refused her sales pitch for a string of sweet-smelling jasmine she would curse you in a shrill voice that drowned the noise of the home-going Hondas, starting with "You number ten cheap Charlie" and ending with her opinion of your pedigree through at least three incestuous generations.

Ti Ti's turf was the Continental Palace Hotel and she lived in the jeep that belonged to the Associated Press, whose writers had more or less adopted her, and who described her in one dispatch:

In addition to limpid almond eyes and a woebegone smile of unquestionable innocence, Ti Ti had the inborn gift of the con. Her strategy was to lurk among the potted plants of the hotel's terrace bar, barefoot in her tattered dress, until a young helicopter pilot or civilian engineer entered with a girl on his arm.

"Frowers for a pletty rady," Ti Ti would intone in her fractured English, pushing a string of fragrant jasmine blossoms under the lady's nose.

If the man refused he was immediately exposed as a "cheap, cheap Charlie" or worse. The abuse grew in volume as the couple moved toward a table and abated only when Ti Ti was paid to go away.

Then when dinner was served on the terrace, Ti Ti would stare hungrily in, like a Third-World famine poster, at the diners.

And as they walked away, usually throwing her a face-saving coin or two, she would occasionally be seen standing on tippy toes to relieve the donor of his watch or ring, which she took for safekeeping to her friend Con Cua, The Crab.

Still, despite Ti Ti and her friends, Saigon was not a bad place to be. The U.S. field observers were filing realistic reports of the war to the U.S. Embassy where nobody seemed to take the slightest notice of them. Ambassador Graham Martin still appeared to believe that Vietnam would turn into a rich little capitalist country with a minor problem of Communist terrorism in its remoter border provinces. But the military attachés from other nations, the British, and especially the Australians, were frank with their gloomy and accurate assessments of the situation.

The TV crews and still cameramen still had to drive miles into the countryside or fly far north to get any really good bang bangs and a writing journalist did just as well by listening to their stories and talking to the military analysts in the safety of Saigon.

Despite the American optimism, it was a story, there was no doubt, of a country that was collapsing quickly, dramatically, and as the later years proved, disastrously.

## CHAPTER 5

# A million dead is a statistic

Nobody really cared much about Cambodia. The Americans bombed the beautiful, gentle land with extraordinary ferocity from 1969 to 1973, then forgot about it. The media remembered the twenty-one men it had left dead in the jungles, or at least their fellow correspondents remembered. The readers and viewers at home couldn't care less so the bureaus either closed, cut down to a single, lonely staffer, or left it all to a local stringer until it became fairly obvious in the spring of 1975 that the capital of Phnom Penh was going to fall to the Khmer Rouge guerrillas.

Only the French, who kept their Agency France Presse correspondents fairly busy, Syd Schanberg of *The New York Times*, and Neil Davis, a young, freelance television cameraman from Tasmania, seemed to care.

Davis lived in Phnom Penh and loved it probably more than his native Australian island. With his baby face, blond curly hair, and a limp from several shrapnel wounds, he was to become the cor-

72

respondents' correspondent as the Cambodian and Vietnam wars ended. In Cambodia he knew everybody and everything. Members of the Lon Nol government whispered in his ear. So did the military attachés of the embassies. The ordinary people, especially the women, seemed to have a particular affection for him. And when the hit-and-run correspondents came back toward the end he shared his information, experience, and advice freely with all of us.

It was a bit unusual, under the media snobbery system, to have a freelance TV cameraman as the dean and chief advisor of the press corps, but Davis was an unusual man. Sensibly he escaped from his beloved Cambodia just before Phnom Penh fell. The Khmer Rouge could have had him singled out for special treatment. He remained in Saigon after that city fell, took the only TV pictures of the Viet Cong tanks rolling into the presidential palace and then he manned the Reuters wire service during the early days of the occupation, sending out some of the most important and dramatic dispatches of the thirty-year war.

Eventually NBC recognized what every correspondent knew about Davis and made him a staff correspondent based in Bangkok. Even now, when he occasionally enters the Foreign Correspondents' Club of Hong Kong, he is mobbed by old friends who love him and by the new wave of less experienced aspirants in Asia who regard him with awe.

Davis and I spent a couple of nights in my hotel room in Phnom Penh, over a bottle of Scotch, while rockets crunched in the distance, discussing the history of Cambodia and trying to guess what was about to happen. Three names kept emerging in the conversation, names I'd never heard before, Khieu Samphan, Ieng Sary, and Saloth Sar, alias Pol Pot. Davis called them the phantoms of the jungle and we talked of them in terms of hope that they might become the saviors of the then corrupt, deeply troubled land.

We were very wrong. These men, isolated in the jungle, saturated with ideology, unaffected by the small advances made by civilization during their lonely decade of struggle and hate, were to become infamous in the next few years as the architects of one of history's most horrible crimes: the mass murder of their own countrymen.

Obviously, nobody with any sense was flying into Cambodia in March, 1975, so when Tony Clifton of *Newsweek* and I booked on the Air Camboge flight from Hong Kong to Phnom Penh we were the only passengers. The rest of the Caravelle jet was occupied by crates of rice and military equipment. But it was Air Camboge's scheduled and much advertised "champagne flight," and there was enough good French champagne on board to serve a full planeload of a hundred people and a full crew of Cambodian flight attendants to look after them.

Consequently when the jet, half of the airline's fleet, swooped and swerved to avoid a rocket attack as we landed at Phnom Penh's Pontechong airport, Clifton and I weren't all that worried about it. We were even somewhat amused by the small group of correspondents who had been covering the rocket attack and who kept yelling at us, "Run, you stupid bastards," as we walked across to the terminal where they were sheltering.

The only correspondent who wasn't scared in Cambodia was Al Rockoff, a photographer who freelanced for the AP and who seemed to be dressed constantly in the same old pair of jeans and dirty T-shirt. Al wasn't scared because he had already been killed.

In 1974, a few months before the fall of Phnom Penh, he was at the front taking pictures when a shell burst near him and riddled his body with shrapnel. One of the old green vans the Cambodians used as ambulances rushed him to a hospital in the capital, but by the time he arrived his heart had stopped.

There are various versions of how long his heart had stopped beating, ranging from ten minutes to half an hour. Nobody will ever know because nobody in the ambulance checked during the long ride.

But as soon as he was admitted to the hospital, already crowded with wounded soldiers, a Scandinavian nurse began to pummel his chest, massage his heart and give him mouth-to-mouth resuscitation.

Almost miraculously Rockoff began to breath again. In a few weeks he had recovered enough to be sent to Bangkok for some rest and he was back in Phnom Penh with his battery of cameras and dressed in the same old jeans and T-shirt a few weeks before the fall.

One morning, as the Khmer Rouge were bombarding the Pontechong airport with rockets and a few were whistling over the city itself, Rockoff joined a group of us sitting around the pool at the old Le Phnom hotel and remarked, after a while, "Well, I think I'll go out to the airport and get a few goods shots." "Jesus Christ, Al," a TV man said. "If you go out there now you're going to be killed."

"Well," said Al Rockoff casually, picking up his cameras, "it wouldn't be for the first time."

The Chinese-made rockets the Khmer Rouge were pouring at a great rate into the airport and less frequently into the center of the sprawling city in those days were psychological as well as physical weapons. They were meant mainly to create fear and they did.

They shot across the sky with a screaming sound and landed with an explosion that could be heard for miles. Their shells contained coils of twisted steel, as sharp as razor blades, which broke into small pieces of corkscrew-shaped shrapnel on impact and literally twisted the guts out of any unfortunate they hit. It was said that once you heard the scream in the sky the rocket was gone so you were safe and the queasy feeling in the stomach and urge to run somewhere, anywhere, were purposeless. But they still frightened the hell out of everyone, except perhaps Al Rockoff.

They usually came in pairs, so that when the photographers—and more occasionally we journalists— jumped in ancient rented cars and drove toward the sound of the first explosion to report on the deaths and damage, we had the fear that we were driving directly into the path of the second rocket.

For some reason we always felt fairly safe at the Le Phnom hotel, although rockets were regularly hitting the Ministry of Information building only a few hundred yards away. The Monorom hotel a little farther south was in a different situation. The Communists appeared to have a bead on it. Two correspondents who could not get rooms at the Le Phnom, Jack Reynolds of NBC and Frank Mariano of ABC, were forced to live on the top floors of the smaller hotel. They were the most nervous of us all.

One afternoon, one of the rockets hit right in the middle of a group of pedicab drivers waiting outside the hotel and ripped eight or ten of them to pieces. Their bodies were in such a mess it was impossible to know how many of them there had been. I was walking nearby when the rocket hit and I jumped in a pedicab and ordered its skinny puller to run toward the noise. He balked like a frightened horse after a few hundred yards but by then we were in sight of the hotel and the carnage outside. Smoke was still pouring from the bodies on the roadway and there was half a body in the small, round, sandbagged bunker where the hotel guard did his duty. Later, Frank Mariano told me he was in the hotel lobby when the rocket hit, saw the guard in the bunker was wounded and ran to help him. But when he tried to lift the guard clear of the sandbags he found himself hugging only the top half of his body. The incident upset him and ABC sent their toughest old hand, Jim Bennett, to replace him. Frank died in California the following year. He was 38.

Soon after the rocket hit at the Monorom I decided it was close to time to leave. Broadcasts from the Khmer Rouge stating that foreign journalists would be considered "enemies of the people" and shot when Phnom Penh was captured helped me make up my mind.

But I had a conscience about two delightfully crazy Canadian girls, Dolly and Anna Charet, who simply refused to abandon the forty-two tiny children they were caring for at the orphanage they called Canada House.

Although they were both scared stiff, because their spotlessly clean and efficient orphanage was not far from the central market, the object of many rocket attacks, they could not be persuaded by me, the Canadian embassy in Thailand or the British embassy in Cambodia to leave their babies in the care of Cambodian nuns and nurses and go home.

They would just stand there in the orphanage, scared, set smiles on their attractive faces, usually holding a baby and bottle, and shake their heads at the suggestion. "I'm going to stand in front of the Khmer Rouge troops if they come and tell them if they kill me they'll be killing our kids as well," Dolly said once. If she had guessed what the Khmer Rouge were to do when they got to Phnom Penh she might have felt differently.

But she meant it. The two well-to-do sisters from Montebello, Quebec, wouldn't listen to anybody. They were, I suppose, brave but they were also impossible. I cabled *The Toronto Star* at one stage suggesting we try to arrange a helicopter lift as a humanitarian stunt to take the girls and their babies (and incidentally me) to Saigon. But there was no reply from the foreign desk.

Weeks later, in the foyer of the Caravelle Hotel in Saigon, a young woman ran to throw her arms around me. She was weeping with excitement and it was a while before I realized it was Dolly. "We made it, Jack," she wept. "We made it. And we've got the kids with us."

She refused to say how she got the children out of Cambodia, putting her fingers to her lips conspiratorially and saying, "Shush." And next day when I saw the two sisters lining their little children up at Saigon's Tan Son Nhut airport for a flight that would eventually take them to Canada, they still refused to say how they arranged the miracle.

It was not easy for me to get out of Cambodia anyway, with or without the two girls. A USAID DC-3 was taking some Americans, including journalists, out on a daily flight to Saigon, but when I suggested at the U.S. embassy I'd like a ride I was told that no consideration was being given at the time to the evacuation of "third-country nationals."

There were still said to be daily flights to Saigon and Bangkok by Air Camboge's single Caravelle jet and an old DC-4 and the airline's downtown terminal was jampacked with Cambodians carrying all they could crush into a few suitcases or string bags. They were willing to risk the rocket-run bus ride from the bunkered terminal to a bunker at Pontechong and then a run across the open tarmac to the aircraft.

I waited on two mornings at the terminal with several other correspondents and the crowd of frightened Cambodians. But the planes never came. The Cambodians drifted away, stoical men with their arms around weeping wives and little wide-eyed children who seemed unaware of what was going on.

78

Twice a grinning clerk re-welcomed me to the now almost empty Le Phnom hotel. And twice the few remaining correspondents booed my return with a mixture of good humor and professional anguish because I was supposed to be "pigeoning" their stories and film to wherever I could have them transmitted.

Except for once in a while, there was no electricity at the Le Phnom in those days. The old air conditioners rattled no more and the big ceiling fans were still. The big rooms with their bare tile floors were like incinerators and writing by candlelight was a sweaty, difficult business. But there was still reasonably good food at the little restaurant near the hotel's swimming pool and some particularly good French wine. There was also the inevitable Asian gaggle of good-looking girls, lounging in deckchairs on the lawn near the pool and smiling enticingly.

As a happily married man I always avoided the women. It was probably easier for me than for some others. To begin with I had had a mild coronary in Hong Kong shortly before this assignment and my doctor had instructed me to avoid any undue stress and excitement. I was not too sure whether a shot of sexual excitement combined with the nervous stress of the overall situation would do me any good. And secondly, I am allergic to penicillin, a disastrous impediment to any active involvement with readily available Asian women.

Perhaps on this night though it was the French wine or just the feeling that life was short and lonely. She was half Chinese and half Cambodian and although she must have been in her mid thirties, she was very beautiful and she acted in that dingy, candlelit hotel room as if it was one of her last nights on earth, which it probably was.

We were exactly at the climax of our short but hectic relationship when a rocket hit about a hundred yards from the hotel, shaking the walls and scattering big, broken bits of ceiling plaster on the bed and the floor. In an instant, while the noise still reverberated and the building still shook, she threw me onto the floor, overturned the bed and pulled me under it, shaking while she hugged me on the cold tiles.

I've been confident ever since I will never have another heart attack. It would have happened then.

I got out of Phnom Penh, well before the city fell, on an Australian Air Force C-130, sent to evacuate Australian embassy personnel, and I was glad to go. Denis Warner, the great Australian expert on Southeast Asia, a journalistic hero of my youth whom I'd never met before, escaped with me. He complained, as an embassy car drove us on a devious route through open fields to the airport, that the older he got the more right-wing were his views, creating a bias that was a journalistic nuisance.

The timing was terrific. The Australians had, of course, brought some beer along but there was time only for one Foster's lager before the big plane touched down on a back section of the airport. The pilots kept the motors running. There were some burned-out skeletons of planes nearby and a wrecked World Airlines DC-8, one of the shuttle that had been bringing American sponsored rice to the besieged city. Two rockets hit the airport as we boarded the plane. We were lumbering off and zig-zagging away within minutes.

Some correspondents stayed. Syd Schanberg of *The New York Times* stayed. He wanted to win a Pulitzer Prize and he did. Claude Juvenal and Jean Jacques Cazeau, of Agence France Presse stayed. They wrote the final stories, the best ones. Young Jon Swain, a freelancer for the London *Sunday Times*, came to my hotel room in Saigon a week or so after I left Cambodia, told me he was thinking of going into Phnom

Penh and asked for my advice. I told him not to go, it would be madness.

"I've got to make a name for myself," he said. "It's the only way the *Sunday Times* will put me on staff." He won the British Journalist of the Year Award for his Cambodia coverage and the *Sunday Times* put him on staff.

Peter Kent of the Canadian Broadcasting Corporation went in, leaving his bags in my hotel room in Saigon for safekeeping, and came out with the American helicopter evacuation as Phnom Penh was falling. So did Tony Paul, of *Reader's Digest*. They were all mad and they all got great stories, but those who bravely stayed to face the Khmer Rouge missed the big one, the fall of Saigon two weeks later.

In the spring of 1976, I went back as close as I could get to Cambodia. The war had been over for a year then. Cambodia was the Democratic Republic of Kampuchea. The phantoms of the jungle were in control. (They, in turn, have since been deposed.) Pathetic refugees were scrambling into Thailand, starving and shot at, separated from their families, flooding the primitive refugee camps with a horrible human mess.

I took Marie with me to the border at Avanyaprathet. I shouldn't have because bandits hit fairly frequently along the 200 miles of highway from Bangkok. But women who are stuck on the rock of Hong Kong for long periods of time seem to suffer a form of claustrophobia and I had thought Marie would agree to remain in Bangkok to buy silks and teapots. She didn't agree and she came.

In the circumstances I checked more carefully than usual, with Peter Collins of CBS and other staff correspondents in Bangkok, on the state of the road. We delayed departure for a day until Mike, the driver of car number five at the Oriental Hotel, who had been highly recommended by Tony Paul, was available. It is an essential part of the art, any experienced foreign correspondent will tell a new chum, to pick a driver who is more scared than you are. This is one of the better guarantees of survival. Mike, of the Oriental's car number five was suitably and sensibly scared.

The suitably scared driver is not concerned much for your safety, of course. You are just a rich nut who wants to go where no sane person would want to go and your stupidity is such that you deserve to be killed. He is scared for his own safety, but more importantly for his car, usually an American model of early 1960s vintage, held together by loving care and bits of wire. This is his lifetime investment and the precious support of his family.

Some drivers in Vietnam, like Hughie, whom I shared with the CBC, had an amazing instinct for survival. Acting on some strange intuition he would pull his old rattletrap off the road and dive into a ditch minutes before a shell exploded anywhere near his source of livelihood, himself and incidentally us.

Only in Beirut, which sent veteran Vietnam correspondents back to Hong Kong heaving huge sighs of relief, and which mercifully I covered only briefly during the 1978 Israeli invasion, does the scared driver rule not apply, and possibly for good reason. In that crazily inhumane mess of hate and rubble the drivers are often so scared they can't function properly at all. They have to be threatened and bullied and the excessive amount of fear some of them exude is offensive, making the car an unpleasant place and the journey "down the road" unduly dangerous because the correspondent has to use his own judgment almost entirely.

Mike, the scared, proud owner-driver of car number 5, took us to Aranyaprathet without incident. He even played soft, European classical music on a stereo system either to soothe himself or us as he picked up speed through the bush-lined sections of the highway where the bandits usually hid. He introduced us to the only restaurant in Aranyaprathet and its only non-rice dish of tough chicken legs, and he booked us into a complex of cottages on the edge of the village. The can was a plastic bucket and a hole in the floor but the cottage was clean.

There were about 3,000 refugees in a camp on the fringes of Aranyaprathet, not far from the border crossing at Poipet, and they were surviving on a ration of two cans of rice a day and a little fish or meat every three days. Big families huddled in tiny squalid spaces behind barbed wire. There was no water supply, but the refugees were allowed to walk once a day to a river about half a mile away to carry water in kerosene cans.

Marie and I were not allowed inside the camp, although some Christian missionaries were. They were distributing T-shirts marked "Jesus Saves" to the Buddhist inmates. Mike, the driver, was allowed to go in and he brought a selection of Cambodians to the guarded gate to meet us.

Korm Kery, fifty-two, the first man who came, couldn't shake hands because his were covered in festering sores, and he could hardly walk because he had been shot three times while escaping. My notes show that he said:

I am a major. I was one of the senior officers in the camp at Battambang when Phnom Penh fell on April 17.

After we surrendered we were put in a school and guarded, of course. On April 22 at 2 P.M. the Khmer Rouge came and said senior officers were to go to Phnom Penh to welcome Prince Sihanouk [the former Cambodian leader who had been in exile in Peking]. We were told to collect our clothes, uniforms and whatever food we had.

At 2:30 P.M. we were told to get into trucks. There were six trucks and a bus. There were 312 of us. We drove in a convoy with Khmer Rouge in a jeep and a Land Rover escorting us about twenty kilometers from Battambang. The convoy turned off the road to Phnom Penh toward a mountain called Tipbodia.

About 200 meters from the foot of the mountain they told us to get off the trucks and rest and the trucks drove away. Then we realized there was going to be an execution of all of us.

Another officer and I ran into the jungle. They fired at us and I was wounded in the arm. There was the sound of guns behind us, machine guns and rifles. The Khmer Rouge were firing from west to east and east to west. The other officers were all caught in the crossfire. I saw them fall down. Then there was just smoke.

We hid for two nights in the jungle then I went back to Battambang to look for my family. I have, or I had, thirteen children aged between two-and-a-half and twenty-four. I hid for three days and nights in a temple and tried to make contact with them, but I learned they had been ordered to leave Battambang.

I ran at night to another village where I pretended I had never been a soldier and I was sent to work in the fields growing rice until February when I heard five ex-soldiers had been caught and shot.

A lot of people were dying, hundreds of them, and I was sick too, so I was taken to hospital for three days. Then I said I was well enough to go back to work but I escaped into the jungle.

I moved at night through the jungle for twelve days. I didn't have anything to eat except roots and leaves. Then when I got near the border they saw me and fired at me. I was shot in the back and an arm and a leg. I was all covered in blood, but I crawled over the border.

I am not well now, but I would like to go back to try to find my family again. I suppose most of them are dead.

Would you tell the free world that Cambodia needs help?

Marie went to the village and bought some streptomycin for the major's festering sores. He was very grateful.

One by one Mike brought more men to the camp gate. Thi Campa-Het was a tough-looking, shy man of twenty-nine, who had been a private in the Cambodian army for a year before Phnom Penh fell. When we talked to him, two months after he escaped to Thailand he still had deep rope burns on his arms. Thi said:

I come from the village of Tuktala, near Sisophon in the northwest. When the Khmer Rouge came I did not say I was a solider. I spent eight months growing rice.

Then, on January 3, the Khmer Rouge put me in jail with about a hundred others. They must have discovered I had been a soldier. I was three days in the jail. They tied our legs with chains, two or three men on each length of chain.

On January 7 they said they were taking us out to grow rice again and they put us into trucks, but they tied our legs with ropes and they bound our arms behind our backs with red nylon rope, which is the sign of death.

There were forty-eight people in the truck I was in and we were driven down Route 5 to a mountain near Poipet. The men in the truck started crying because they knew what was going to happen.

Near a temple near the mountain some of the Khmer Rouge, five of them, got off the truck and started to walk behind. I managed to get my legs a bit loose and a man in front of me got his arms completely untied. I signalled to him that I was sitting on an iron bar and to hit the one Khmer Rouge still on the truck with it.

He hit the Khmer Rouge on the head with the iron bar and we both jumped off the truck and crawled into the jungle. I got my feet loose and was able to run. They shot at me but missed. I ran about a hundred meters, lay down, and looked back to see what the Khmer Rouge was doing. I could not see for the smoke but many guns were firing and people were crying and screaming.

Gradually over two days, as Mike brought out more and more refugees, the horrible enormity of the story of Cambodia after the war unfolded. The refugees told of an occurrence perhaps without precedence in history, of a whole country turned into a giant, moving *gulag*, of a people terrorized and driven into unpaid work gangs, families purposely split, denied food and sex, moving across the country to wherever labor was required, dying on the roads from exhaustion or execution, dropping dead from disease or starvation in the paddy fields.

They drew a picture of a strange new society, run by the former phantoms of the jungle, now known mysteriously as the *Angka Loeu*—the Organization on High.

It was a society that had no monetary system, no schools, transportation, telephones, electricity, shops, private property: only the long lines of forced, unpaid labor in the paddy fields and death for the weak, the educated and the ideologically incompatible. It was no less than an attempt to create a new man, faithful to the thoughts of the Organization on High, by killing the old and the unconvertible, often with clubs because bullets were scarce. It was a genocide, enormous and ugly and unknown to the rest of the world.

A U.S. State Department specialist, Kenneth M. Quinn, had written with remarkable perception in 1974 that the Communist Khmer Rouge had committed themselves to "total social revolution which would be accomplished by psychologically reconstructing individual members of society.

"This process," he wrote, "entails stripping away, through terror and other means, the traditional bases, structures and forces which have shaped and guided an individual's life until he is left as an atomized, isolated unit; and then rebuilding him according to party doctrine by substituting a series of new values, organizations and ethical norms."

Nobody at the time, of course, believed such nonsense. But we did as I interviewed the refugees at Aranyaprathet and Marie shuttled back and forth from the village bringing more antibiotics for the open sores and rotting limbs of the lucky survivors.

Part of the story of the cruel, complete evacuation of Phnom Penh, and of all the other cities of Cambodia, were told by the correspondents who stayed to cover the Khmer Rouge victory and saw the start of it from their refuge in the French embassy. But the full story was not known until these surviving dregs of the disaster began to talk in the Thai refugee camps.

After hundreds of similar interviews, before and after mine, mainly in the camp at Aranyaprathet, Tony Paul and John Barron pieced the terrible evacuation story together and wrote in their book, *Murder of a Gentle Land*:

Inexplicably, the communists concentrated initially upon expelling the sick and wounded from hospitals which were jammed with fresh casualties of the last bombardment. Troops stormed into the Preah Ket Melea Hospital, Phnom Penh's largest and oldest, and shouted to patients, physicians and nurses alike, "Out! Everybody out! Get out!" They made no distinction between bedridden and ambulatory patients, between the convalescing and the dying, between those awaiting surgery and those who had just undergone surgery. Hundreds of men, women and children in pajamas limped, hobbled, struggled out of the hospital into the streets where the midday sun had raised the temperature to well over 100 degrees Fahrenheit. Relatives or friends pushed the beds of patients too wounded, crippled or enfeebled to walk, some holding aloft perfusion bottles dripping plasma or serum into the bodies of loved ones. One man carried his son, whose legs had just been amputated. The bandages on both stumps were red with blood, and the son, who appeared to be about twenty-two, was screaming, "You can't leave me like this! Kill me! Please kill me!"

Ang Sokthan, 22, was a pharmacy student at the University of Phnom Penh when the city fell. She was a pretty girl but painfully thin when I interviewed her in Aranyaprathet. Sometimes as we talked, she tried to smile, but she couldn't make it. Instead, tears welled into her big brown eyes. This is her story.

On the day Phnom Penh fell, at about 5 P.M. some Khmer Rouge soldiers came to our house and told us we would have to leave the city because the United States was going to come back and bomb it. Our parents were not in Phnom Penh, so I walked with my brother Savin, who was twenty-six, an engineer, my brother Sokun, who was twenty-four, a student in electronics, and my sister Sokphal, who was twenty, a

88

high school student, until we were about a kilometer from the outskirts of the city.

There were thousands of people on the road and dead people beside the road. We were very tired so we stayed the night in a temple and in the morning we marched again. We walked for another three days and then asked the Khmer Rouge if we could rest because one of the other women we had met on the way was having a baby and they let us rest for a while.

It was very terrible. We had had no food at all and we had walked for three days and three nights. They let us stop for a while at a village called Batheby about forty kilometers from Phnom Penh.

Next day my sister and I were made to walk across the rice paddies for about ten kilometers and put to work making a dam. We had never done any manual work before and our job was to carry heavy loads of soil in baskets to make a dam.

We did this for three months, working from 5 A.M. to 10:30 P.M. and sometimes longer on nights when the moon was out. It was very terrible. Even if it was raining we had to keep on working.

At first we were given a small tin can and a half of rice per person per day, but after a month the rice ran out and we were fed little bits of corn and after another month all we got was berries. People were very sick. When they fainted from hunger or malaria they were taken back to the village. We slept in a tent and we were very unhappy. We had no soap to clean ourselves and I lost a lot of weight.

After three months, one morning at 1 A.M., the Khmer Rouge said all the people working on the dam would have to move to another village, so we walked a long way through the night and were taken by truck to a station and then by train to Sisophon, near the Thai border. There was no food or water on the train, but we met our brothers who had been working the rice paddies and were very sick from starvation and malaria. My brothers were taken to a hospital in a school. It was filthy. There was just one potion kept in used penicillin bottles and given to all patients no matter what was wrong with them. Most of the "doctors" and other hospital staff were illiterate.

My sister and I were sent out to make another dam, but this time we had to work waist-deep in the water and we got only half a can of rice a day and sometimes two extra cans of unhusked rice. After a while the Khmer Rouge came and told us our brothers were seriously sick and we could go to the hospital to look after them.

The hospital had one "doctor" then and was full of people with diarrhea and malaria and people with swollen bodies from malnutrition. A lot of them were dying, dozens of them. My brother Savin died first and then my brother Sokun a week later. They were buried in a field without any ceremony or anything, just as if they were animals.

I decided then it was best to die quickly by a bullet rather than slowly like all the other people. So, soon after that—it was in November—my sister and I escaped from Sisophon with thirty others and walked for three nights toward the border until I couldn't walk any farther. My foot was cut by thorns and I kept falling down. I told my sister and a man who was with us to go ahead and I lay down in the jungle to die. But I felt better after a while and wandered by myself in the jungle following the sun for eight days without anything to eat. I licked dew from leaves to try to stop the thirst.

On the ninth morning I woke up near a cow trail near a village. I hoped it was maybe in Thailand. There were two men on the trail and I ran out and grabbed the older man by the hand and said, "I've just escaped from Cambodia!" The younger man asked, "Is she human?" He spoke in Thai; I knew I was free.

Only eight of the thirty who set out from Sisophon got across the border and some of them told me my sister must have died near the border. They said they had heard an explosion or gunshot and had found a dead girl.

I was very sick but I feel better now.

She tried to smile again, but she couldn't.

The stories poured out as Mike brought the pathetic, lucky refugees to the gate. Bodies rotting on the roadsides or thrown into rivers, ruining the drinking water. Young women, probably prostitutes, bludgeoned to death with blows to the back of the head. Bodies of children, one every two hundred yards on some parts of some roadways, dead from dehydration. Loved ones hacked to death with hoes. A large group of women on a cart track east of Khal Kabei, buried up to their necks, their throats stabbed, their heads swollen with putrefaction.

At that time, in the spring of 1976, a year after the fall of Phnom Penh, I made a rough, very unscientific guess at the number killed in the genocide. I simply subtracted from the total population of Cambodia, which had been more than seven million, the twenty to thirty percent those I interviewed said they knew to have been executed or died from disease or starvation. I wrote a story stating there were more than a million dead.

"Was it Stalin," Marie asked sadly as I was pounding the typewriter, "who said a single death is a tragedy but a million deaths is a statistic?"

Anthony Paul and John Barron, after much more careful research, estimated that 1.2 million men, women, and children died in Cambodia between April 17, 1975, and December 1976, as a consequence of the actions of the *Angka Loeu*. Father Francois Ponchaud, a priest who had originally been a Khmer Rouge sympathizer, interviewed thousands of refugees after his escape from Phnom Penh. He put the figure at closer to two million.

But the world didn't care much. In North America, foreign coverage was concentrated on the Middle East and Africa. A few countries, Britain, America, Canada, and Norway, kicked up a bit of a fuss at the United Nations Human Rights Commission. Amnesty International asked for an investigation, and a few organizations and individuals in the western world reacted with shock and horror, but in general the crimes of the Organization on High rated only a few paragraphs every now and again in the papers.

The People's Republic of Kampuchea was a tightly closed country so the TV cameras couldn't take pictures. In the new media era, if there aren't any pictures, stories don't get on the TV newscasts, so they just don't happen. And the world was sick and tired of the troubles of Southeast Asia and Indochina anyway.

After we had done dozens of interviews at the refugee camp, we drove to the bridge at Poipet, the tumbledown metal and wood structure that separates Thailand from Cambodia. From the Thai side we could see black-suited Khmer Rouge soldiers a few hundred yards away unloading crates of liquor from U.S. Army trucks. Thais on motorcycles and on foot were moving on trails through the jungle, apparently using another crossing of the narrow river which we couldn't see, carrying gasoline in every kind of container imaginable, from bottles and jugs to kerosene cans and oil drums into Cambodia, and returning with cases of bottles of good French wine and Johnny Walker Red Label Scotch.

I fitted a 200 mm lens to my Nikon and walked along the bridge to take pictures of this operation and especially of the Khmer Rouge soldiers. Mike and

Marie yelled at me to come back and they hid behind a concrete bridge pylon. Through the long distance lens I could see the Khmer soldiers aiming rifles at me. But they didn't shoot.

For some personal, emotional reason I wanted to defy this new man, these automats created by the Organization on High in the land that used to be so lovely, so I continued to walk until I was just more than halfway across the bridge, clicking the camera, watching the men in the black pajamas run and hide from the little lens that could turn the eyes of the outside world upon them and their ignorance. They ran behind bushes and posts and trucks and raised their rifles but they didn't fire.

It was a stupid, unprofessional thing to do. They were too far away even for the long distance lens. I knew the pictures wouldn't be much good and eventually the paper didn't use them. But for some reason, as I walked back across the bridge into Thailand, I felt better.

"You're crazy, sir," Mike said gently when I was safely back on solid Thai soil and he hustled me quickly into his car.

## CHAPTER 6

# Flight from Da Nang

In the Central Highlands and northern provinces of South Vietnam more than a million people took to the roads early in 1975, some for the third or fourth time, pushing their pathetically few worldly possessions on carts or on bikes southward, in one of history's great exoduses.

Their panic was contagious and cumulative. Some said they abandoned their towns and villages because they feared they would be killed by the Communists and some said they left because government officials had told them to leave. Most of them said they left simply because everybody else was leaving in a panic. Not one of the hundreds I talked to said they had left because of a love of freedom or because of loyalty to the constitutional government of President Thieu. And not all of them fled. In the two-thirds of the country already controlled by the Communists at least six of the eight million people remained, giving some credence to the Communists' claim that they commanded the loyalty of the majority of the people.

But those who did flee left towns and villages simultaneously undefended and unconquered, with the retreat outpacing the offensive by many days, so the streets of the towns were eerily empty and silent. The refugees clogged the narrow roads to the coast in an endless pathetic procession we called the "trail of tears." They became, those who survived, the first of the "boat people," who continued the exodus in leaky craft, either drowning or scattering themselves on the coasts of Thailand, Malaysia, Indonesia, and even far away Australia, where they were virtually forgotten for almost five years. Then the richer, more sophisticated, ethnic Chinese community of Vietnam began their more visible flight in bigger boats. The TV cameras were able to capture the escapes of the more publicity conscious Chinese. Space for their stories suddenly became available in the newspapers. Statistics were transformed into real people and belatedly the world began to care.

The correspondents based in Saigon knew the war was over when the northern imperial capital of Hue, the spiritual center of the country, with its emperor's tombs, fell without a fight on March 26, 1975. This created yet another exodus of civilians, but mainly of soldiers, abandoning their weapons, shoving civilians aside on the roads. They scrambled for boats, under contemptuous Communist fire, to take them down the coast to Da Nang, the second biggest city of South Vietnam.

Hue fell so suddenly it caught all of us in the comparative comfort of Saigon or out on the coastal roads with the earlier refugees, so that one of the biggest stories of the Vietnam war was virtually uncovered. Peter Arnett, of Associated Press, the old pro who won a Pulitzer Prize for his war coverage, made an attempt to get in to Hue from Da Nang with two Vietnamese NBC cameramen, but their jeep could not move against the stream of refugees pouring through the Hai Van Pass not far from Da Nang. Anyway, the bridges on the road were blown away so they had to turn back. Paul Vogle, the skinny, affable, hard-drinking correspondent of UPI, who speaks perfect Vietnamese, managed to talk his way onto a rescue helicopter and landed in Hue briefly to record some of the panicky evacuation scene, but that was all.

And it was not easy to get into Da Nang. The Air Vietnam commercial flights out of the city were naturally packed with richer refugees, and for some inexplicable reason the flights in were also booked out for days ahead. It was too far and too dangerous to travel by road. In the circumstances, the lonely newspaper journalist, who has no logistical backup and no funds to charter planes or choppers, has to call in a few debts. ABC owed me a few for "pigeoning" film out of Cambodia, or somewhere. I had forgotten where, but their crews remembered, and in their cluttered Saigon bureau headquarters, a room at the Caravelle Hotel, we made a deal.

They had chartered a plane to deliver film to a cameraman in Nha Trang, halfway up the coast to Da Nang, but the pilot was scared and unreliable. His old aircraft had two engines but it was also unreliable, they pointed out. But if I would make sure their film was delivered at Nha Trang, I could take the plane on to Da Nang, provided, of course, the pilot would go on.

The pigeoning system was one of the nicer things about covering the wars or, for that matter, any of the troublesome stories, where correspondents lived and worked together in difficult circumstances. The competition, particularly between the TV networks and the wire services, was always intense, but there was a general understanding that anybody moving toward any efficient communications facility would carry and file anybody else's film or stories.

In Phnom Penh there was even an official pigeon roster, essentially for the wire services and TV networks, for running the gauntlet of rockets pounding the airport. A correspondent for an individual newspaper could repay some of the debts he owed for transportation and protection by the TV crews or for access to the wire services copy, by volunteering to take his turn carrying the daily bundle to a departing aircraft.

Once, in Saigon, I heard that CBS was chartering an Air Vietman 707 jet to fly a single bag of film to Hong Kong. I heard about it because the CBS crews were highly and vocally annoyed about the fact that the government airline would charter only its luxury jet, with a full first-class crew and extra stewardesses, at an additional cost of several thousand dollars.

"No use wasting all that space," I told the CBS bureau chief, Brian Ellis, who was a good friend. "I've got a roll of film that has to get to Toronto." So my single little Kodak cassette won the only other occupied seat on the large plane to Hong Kong, where the CBS staff shipped it immediately to Toronto. The pictures were in the paper less than twenty-four hours after I had taken them.

But when I arrived at Than Son Nhut airport to board the ABC's charter to Nha Trang and on to Da Nang it was difficult to believe that my past efforts at pigeoning had paid off this time. The small monoplane was at least forty years old. One wing appeared to be attached to the fuselage with what looked like old, unbent, coat hangers. The pilot was at least sixty, probably sixty-five years old. He peered at his charts from about an inch away, as if he was almost blind. And he spoke only French. I had been wondering why Jim

Bennett, the toughest of the ABC correspondents who was himself trying to get into Da Nang, had not taken advantage of this ABC charter, and as I climbed into the cockpit beside the ancient pilot, the reason dawned on me. Bennett is a survivor.

We got off the ground, however, taking up an amazing amount of Tan Son Nhut's long runway in the process, and we got to Nha Trang and assumed that we delivered the film. Helicopters were landing at the airport, disgorging unarmed soldiers and a few civilians from the trail of tears. But the terminal buildings were ghostly quiet and the parts of the once beautiful seaside city we could see appeared to have been abandoned. The old pilot opened doors and shouted at each of the airport's empty buildings until finally a Vietnamese emerged from one of them and agreed to accept the film.

He said he knew where the stringer was, although he seemed to me to be confused about whether the man worked for ABC or NBC. In any event he knew a television cameraman who probably needed film and this was good enough for the old French pilot. When I tried to argue that we should personally deliver the film, he climbed into his funny old plane and revved its engines ominously. He did agree to fly on to Da Nang, though, over beaches on which small groups of refugees huddled, skirting carefully around the black smoke from several artillery battles, but when we were over Da Nang he talked briefly with the control tower and refused to land.

I shouted at him in English: "Put the thing down, you old bastard. You're going to have to get gas anyway."

"*La guerre est là,*" he shouted back. "*Impossible.*"

The runway looked peaceful and empty enough so I grabbed the control column and pushed it forward. I was stronger than he was so he landed the thing. He didn't bother about getting gas. He didn't even cut his engine. He was supposed to wait for me but as soon as I stepped onto the tarmac he took off. It was lonely standing in the center of the big, empty tarmac, but I was glad he was gone.

Jim Bennett was in the terminal, having somehow wangled a place on a commercial flight, with two other American correspondents who had chartered a plane. Peter Arnett had returned to Da Nang after his unsuccessful attempt to get into Hue and he and Bruce Wilson of the Melbourne *Herald* were trying to get out. They briefed us innocents on the events of the last few hours.

Hue had completely collapsed and the refugees and routed soldiers were pouring into downtown Da Nang. There were rumors that some of the leaders of the 1st Infantry Division, had been killed when a helicopter was shot down just south of the city. A rocket attack on the air base had killed six people and wounded thirty-four in the slums on the base's periphery.

Arnett, the most experienced of the Vietnam correspondents, who had long since earned his epaulets for courage and wisdom, told me: "This is no place to be, Jack. It's time to get out. The war is over, up here at least."

But we couldn't get out. Arnett and Wilson and a TV crew had the last seats on the last plane. It was hot and the terminal was packed with the leftovers from this last flight out, but the stall selling the usual warm beer and chunk of dirty ice was still open. I found a space at a table and rattled off the story as Wilson had told it to me while I drank three dirty, cooling beers and Wilson almost missed the plane in his wait to pigeon out for me what was really his own story.

Bennett's local Vietnamese crew had a jeep so the four of us who were left behind drove downtown and

99

checked in to the Grande Hotel on the waterfront. There were huge crowds of refugees on the docks and disheveled, obviously completely demoralized soldiers were pouring ashore from big landing barges, sometimes pushing the civilians aside. There was no panic and not much noise except for the occasional sound of a three-wheeled Lambretta bus, disgorging more refugees, with their most precious possessions, their sewing machines, radios, and baskets of fruit and rice. Mostly there was a strange, dazed silence in downtown Da Nang, and we were the only guests at the Grande Hotel.

We had just checked in when John Swenson, of the U.S. Information Service told us to check out again. "Full evacuation," he said. "Everybody out including newsmen. I don't know how you got here, but you've got to go. We'll have a plane in to take you out tonight. Meanwhile you're forbidden to leave the hotel."

We sat around in the bar for a while and when Swenson went back to the consulate I walked down to the docks to interview refugees and take pictures.

The docks were crowded with people, the streets as well, mostly women, squatting quietly under their conical hats, feeding their children or just waiting for something, anything, to happen. But there was no panic. Swenson was annoyed when I got back to the hotel, but I had four rolls of good film so I didn't care much and when he handed out pieces of paper, which were supposed to be passes for the evacuation flight, he gave me mine along with the others and a stern remark that I was lucky to get one.

We took the jeeps to the airport at 7:30 P.M. and waited for the World Airlines plane in a bunker outside the main airport gate as we had been instructed. There seemed to be nobody else around except a few army helicopter pilots who begged us to try to take them and their families with us.

Then the plane landed and people emerged from everywhere, from buildings and behind bushes, and out of the sandbagged bunkers and they crowded around the gate. There was still no real panic until a U.S. embassy employee in civilian clothes (probably a CIA man) stationed inside the gate, began to fire his pistol in the air.

Bennett, who had been sipping at a bottle of Johnny Walker in our bunker and who gets angry easily anyway, shouted at the man to stop it. Two of us tried to talk to him but he pointed the pistol at us and then went on firing it in the air.

"You stupid bastard," Bennett was shouting. "Stop it you stupid bastard. You'll cause a panic." The man didn't stop and there was a panic, thanks partly to him.

The mass of people, perhaps a thousand of them, some waving pieces of paper the same as ours, pushed through the gate or crawled under the wires and mobbed the aircraft. U.S. officials allowed some of them on board. I had to try to console a woman who tried over and over again to break through a cordon of armed U.S. soldiers. Her five children had been taken on board the plane but she had not made it. Her wails were so piercing and continuous they rose above the noise of the engines of the huge jet. I talked to the soldiers and they escorted her onto the plane so she could take her children off. She was smiling when she walked away from the plane with them, back to the danger of Da Nang.

The plane was about half full when the pilot ordered the doors closed and the gangways removed. He taxied through the panicky mob and took off for Cam Ranh Bay. The U.S. consul-general drove us back through the eerily silent, crowded city to the Grande Hotel.

In situations like this there is a correspondents' hierarchy and it is usually the correspondent in charge of a TV crew who takes a leadership role and, for some reason, if there are several network crews it is the CBS man. Bruce Dunning of CBS, a quiet ex-newspaper-man based in Tokyo, called us together in the deserted bar of the deserted hotel and announced in one of the quaint phrases that afflict TV men: "We're going to have to activate the charter."

I'd heard about the charter. It was an old propellor-driven C-46 which the networks and wire services had standing by in Saigon, in a cooperative deal, in case any of their staff found themselves in serious trouble they couldn't get out of. It was costing a lot of money but nobody had used it through the fall of Phnom Penh and the start of the collapse of South Vietnam.

"I can't use the charter," I said. "*The Toronto Star* hasn't paid any of the shot. We're not in on the deal." Again it was difficult working for an individual newspaper with no logistical backup.

"It's OK," Dunning said. "We'll take you along as a refugee."

To get in touch with the CBS bureau in Saigon he had to get to the U.S. consulate. He took the risky walk through the unsettled city streets, now filled with angry, disillusioned, and disorganized soldiers, some of them robbing and looting, in the middle of the night. He is short and tubby and he was sweating when he got back, not entirely from the heat.

"There was one emergency line still open. They let me use it and I activated the charter," he said. "One o'clock tomorrow at the airport."

In the morning Da Nang, though crowded, was still reasonably quiet. The refugees and soldiers, hun-

dreds and thousands of them, were still packed
pathetically on the docks, bargaining in exorbitant
amounts with ferrymen to take them to the ships in the
river. The normal population of the city was 458,000.
Now it was more than double that. There was some
pushing and shoving to get on the sampan ferries, but
not much. Vietnamese boy scouts politely and effec-
tively patrolled the docks, helping keep order.

We had breakfast at the street stalls outside the
hotel, dry bread and coffee which was all there was,
and the jeeps arrived about 11 A.M. to take us to the
airport. As I checked out of the hotel, the biggest in Da
Nang, the owner, a well-dressed woman wearing
dainty brocade slippers with turned-up toes, took my
money then burst into tears and began to babble
hysterically in Vietnamese.

A boy from a stall interpreted for me. "She wants
to go with you," he said.

She took a bundle of money from the till, stuffed it
in a little handbag, locked the doors of the hotel and
climbed into one of the jeeps beside the eighty-year-
old mother of one of the Vietnamese sound men.

The city was still quiet as we drove the first few
blocks from the waterfront and then it suddenly seized
up. Traffic, cars, jeeps, motorcycles, Lambretta buses,
and bullock carts clogged the narrow streets and
crashed into each other at intersections. People were
packed so tightly on the pavements, pushing against
each other, trying to move in different directions, it
was next to impossible to move anywhere. It was hot
and the sweat soaked my bushjacket.

We abandoned the jeeps but still couldn't move
through the people. Fuch, the AP cameraman, with
only half a face as a result of a front-line assignment a
few years previously, flailed about with his cameras
trying to force a passage through the mob. W. B.
Tang, the diminutive Chinese ABC cameraman and

103

his equally tiny soundman, Dinh, were loaded down with huge amounts of heavy equipment, and they used it like protective armor to charge into the crowd and clear a way for me and Dinh's mother, who seemed to be quite calm about the whole thing. Little Tang must have thought I was having trouble staying with them and maybe I was. He took my fairly heavy camera bag, adding it to the great weight he was already carrying. We left a few people spreadeagled in the gutters, but we made it to a clear space and a soldier on a Honda took me on his pillion to the airport.

There were at least 100,000 people at the airport, trying to climb over high wire fences to get to the runway. Some made it and some didn't. Their clothes were torn. Some abandoned their shoes near the fences so they could grip the wires with bare toes. A few American officials tried to keep order.

The soundman's ancient mother was there, smiling and not even sweating, and the hotel owner, clutching her purse full of piastres. We showed the passes Swenson had given us the previous night and the Americans allowed all of our group onto the runway.

There had been some World Airways flights to Nha Trang during the morning, but they had all been mobbed by the crowds, mostly by soldiers, so now the flights had been canceled. An executive of the airline warned us that our plane would be mobbed too if it arrived. He went to the control tower, contacted our pilot, told him to land on a remote section of the strip, and be ready to take off immediately. We gathered our small group together, walked to the part of the strip he had indicated and we waited.

But the word spread and our group somehow grew bigger, to maybe a hundred people. When the old C-46 landed, they rushed it, its motors still roaring, so that we all had to punch and elbow our way aboard. Others on the tarmac, mostly soldiers and their families, jumped into jeeps and on Hondas when they saw the plane land and sped toward it, surrounding it with a yelling, panicky cordon. The plane was grossly overloaded with about 150 people and we had to push others, pathetically, off the plane's ladder, sending them sprawling to the tarmac. A young woman hurled a tiny baby into my arms as the plane began to move and we were trying to pull in the ladder and close the door.

"Take him, please take him," she wailed in English. I didn't know what to do with the baby so we stopped the plane briefly and pulled the mother on board. We staggered off with our load, followed the length of the tarmac by jeeps and Hondas carrying people waving fists at us.

We thought we were the last correspondents in downtown Da Nang before it collapsed in complete panic and was captured, two days later, by two truckloads of guerrillas, about half of them women. We put in our stories that we were. But Brian Barron, the BBC TV correspondent, and his crew had managed somehow to penetrate the panic into the downtown area as we were leaving, to take some of the best film footage of the war and eventually escape on one of the refugee ships. The few remaining Americans in the city where the United States had first entered the fighting ten years before with a marine assault on the beaches, also escaped ignominiously by ship. The incredibly calm consul-general was one of the last to leave, wading and swimming to a ship through the heavy surf, clutching General Ngoc Quang Truong, the commander of the South Vietnamese 1st Infantry Division, who couldn't swim.

Ed Daly, the unpopular president of World Airways, was in many ways a leading actor in this dismal drama of the last days of the American presence in Da Nang. He had decided, this hard-drinking, tough-talking, gun-toting millionaire, to do something personally about the problems of Vietnam. His planes and their courageous crews had been hired first for the U.S. government's rice runs into Phnom Penh when it was beseiged by the Khmer Rouge, then for the refugee flights from Da Nang. They had kept Phnom Penh alive a little longer and they did manage to rescue some of the Da Nang refugees.

The Melbourne *Herald*'s Bruce Wilson once wrote of Daly: "Mr. Ed . . . is not personable. He has a face like a red beacon fed by a hundred bulbs, thirty of which have ceased operation."

Once, at a formal dinner and press conference at the Caravelle Hotel in Saigon, Daly took a pistol from his clothing, placed it beside him at the head table and proclaimed that he would "shoot the next God-damned man who talks while I'm talking." We stopped our chatter at the correspondents' table and walked out on him in disgust.

But Daly had his heroic side as well, and his staff loved him. The day after we activated the charter and escaped from Da Nang, he decided to defy the bureaucracy's order against any further flights and make just one more attempt. His chief pilot, Ken Healy, roared one of the World Airways 727s illegally off Saigon's Tan Son Nhut strip about noon on March 29 and headed for Da Nang, followed by a backup plane, ignoring the chances that fighters would be scrambled to knock them out of the sky. Daly himself was on board the first plane. So were a handful of journalists. Only the major American news organizations were warned of the flight so I heard nothing about it until I read Paul Vogle's story on the UPI wire, one of the most memorable stories of the Vietnam war. (The actual copy, as it came off the UPI machine, is reproduced in the photo section of this book.)

Only the fastest, the strongest, and the meanest of a

huge mob got a ride on the last plane from Da Nang Saturday.

People died trying to get aboard and others died when they fell thousands of feet into the sea because even desperation could no longer keep their fingers welded to the undercarriage.

It was a flight into hell, and only a good, tough American pilot and a lot of prayers got us back to Tan Son Nhut air base alive—with the Boeing 727 flaps jammed and the wheels fully extended.

It was a ride I'll never forget.

World Airways President Ed Daly was aboard. He was angry and tired. Daly said he had been up all night arguing with American and Vietnamese officials for permission to fly into beseiged Da Nang to get some more refugees out.

Daly finally said to hell with paperwork, clearances, and caution and we were on our way.

It seemed peaceful enough as we touched down at the airport 370 miles northeast of Saigon.

Over a thousand people had been waiting around a Quonset hut several hundred yards away from where we touched down.

Suddenly it was a mob in motion. They roared across the tarmac on motorbikes, Jeeps, Lambretta scooters, and on legs speeded by sheer desperation and panic.

Ed Daly and I stood near the bottom of the 727's tail ramp. Daly held out his arms while I shouted in Vietnamese, "One at a time, one at a time. There's room for everybody."

There wasn't room for everybody and everybody knew damn well there wasn't.

Dally and I were knocked aside and backward.

If Ed Daly thought he'd get some women and children out of Da Nang he was wrong. The plane was jammed in an instant with troops of the 1st Division's meanest unit, the *Hac Bao* (Black Panthers).

They literally ripped the clothes right off Daly along with some of his skin. I saw one of them kick an old woman in the face to get aboard.

In the movies somebody would have shot the bastard and helped the old lady on the plane. This was no movie. The bastard flew and the old lady was tumbling down the tarmac, her fingers clawing toward a plane that was already rolling.

A British cameraman who flew up with us made the mistake of getting off the plane when we landed, to shoot the loading.

He could not get back aboard in the pandemonium. In the very best tradition of the business he threw his camera with its precious film into the closing door and stood there and watched the plane take off . . .

As we started rolling, insanity gripped those who had missed the last chance. Government troops opened fire on us. Somebody lobbed a hand grenade toward the wing. The explosion jammed the flaps full open and the undercarriage at full extension.

Communist rockets began exploding at a distance.

Our pilot, Ken Healy, 52, of Oakland, Calif., slammed the throttles open and lurched into the air from the taxiway. There was no way we could have survived the gunfire and got onto the main runway.

A backup 727 had flown behind us but had been ordered not to land when the panic broke out. Its pilot radioed that he could see the legs of people hanging down from the undercarriage of our plane.

UPI photographer Lien Huong, who was in the cockpit of that backup plane, saw at least one person lose his grip on life and plummet into the South China Sea below.

There were 268 or more people jammed into the cabin of the little 727 limping down the coast, only two women and one baby among them. The rest were soldiers, toughest of the tough, meanest of the mean. They proved it today. They were out. They said nothing. They didn't talk to each other or us. They looked at the floor.

I saw one of them had a clip of ammunition and asked him to give it to me. He handed it over. As I walked up the aisle with the clip, other soldiers started loading my arms with clips of ammunition, pistols, hand grenades. They didn't need them anymore. In the cockpit we wrapped the weapons and ammo in electrical tape.

There was no more fight left in the Black Panthers this day.

They had gone from humans to animals and now they were vegetables.

We flew down the coast, the backup plane behind us all the way. Healy circled Phan Rang air base, 165 miles northeast of Saigon, hoping to put down for an emergency landing.

On the backup plane Lien Huong served as interpreter, radioing Phan Rang control tower that the Boeing had to land there in an emergency. The reply came back that there was no fire fighting equipment at Phan Rang so Healy aimed the plane for Tan Son Nhut.

I heard Healy on the radio, telling Tan Son Nhut, "I've got control problems." The backup plane was shepherding us in.

Huong, in the cockpit of the backup plane, told me later when we touched down safe, the pilot and cabin crew on his plane pulled off their headphones, some of them crossed themselves and all thanked God for a small miracle delivered this Easter weekend.

When we touched down the troops who had stormed us were offloaded and put under arrest. They deserved it.

A mangled body of one soldier, M16 rifle still strapped to his shoulder, was retrieved from the undercarriage. He got his ride to Saigon, but being dead in Saigon is just the same as being dead in Da Nang.

Over a score of others came out of the baggage compartment, cold but alive. Somebody told me that four others crawled out of the wheel wells alive. One died.

The last plane from Da Nang was one hell of a ride. For me. For Ed Daly. For Ken Healy. For the Black Panthers. And for two women and a baby.

But the face that remains is that of the old woman lying flat on the tarmac seeing hope, seeing life itself, just off the end of her fingertips and rolling the other way.

Tom Aspin, of Viznews, who threw his camera and film onto the plane as he was being left behind in Da Nang, eventually climbed into the deserted control tower, pressed every button on every instrument and shouted: "Help. I'm all by myself in Da Nang." Somewhere he had pushed the right button. An Air America helicopter landed and carried him to safety.

The CBS bureau held his film for him. There was only a few hundred feet of it. It wasn't much good and it didn't make the air.

CHAPTER 7

# The end of Saigon

Most of the Western correspondents in Southeast Asia in 1975 saw the fall of two regimes: the Lon Nol government in Cambodia had lost most of its American support in 1973 and its capital city, Phnom Penh, fell to the Communist Khmer Rouge forces on April 17, 1975.

Three weeks earlier, in South Vietnam, Hue had fallen to the North Vietnamese troops as they advanced southward toward the capital. We had all known since the beginning of April that Saigon was about to fall and the war would be over. Soon after Da Nang collapsed on March 29, the sprawling, overpopulated city of Saigon, untouched by enemy fire since the Tet offensive of 1968, was surrounded by ten divisions with six more stationed behind them, ready to plug any gaps in the offensive. The Communists' crack troops formed a circle around Saigon, nowhere more than thirty-five miles away.

The people of Saigon knew too and they were scared. I walked into the South Vietnam government tourist bureau on Tu Do Street one afternoon on the off

111

chance that there might be some crazy tourists around who would make a light story, but, of course, there weren't. The building was deserted and the girl behind the counter was doing business in reverse.

"Please take me with you to Canada," she pleaded. "I am very much afraid. My family is from the north and we are all going to be killed. You must be able to arrange to get us out somehow." She was crying and her hands were shaking and she was indeed very much afraid.

The fear was quiet, unpanicky, but it was deep and everywhere. Some committed suicide. Ian Wilson, the CBC's cameraman, who occupied a corner suite at the Caravelle, was woken one morning by the commotion of a suicide in the square below. He jumped from bed, grabbed his camera, flung open the windows, climbed to the ledge and began shooting. He wondered for a while why the crowd below, especially the women, concentrated their attention on him instead of the suicide scene. Then he realized he was wearing only his camera.

Walking the streets was not nice during the last weeks. The beggars were more aggressive, the girls more desperate, and the pickpockets operated almost openly. One day one of them, a girl, approached me as I walked along Tu Do to file a story and announced frankly after she bumped into me, "Excuse me, sir, but I'm a pickpocket." I patted all of my pockets to see what was gone, but they were still buttoned down so I let her go. She had taken my reading glasses from the unbuttoned pocket on the bush jacket sleeve.

There may be nothing more pathetic than a professional observer without his glasses, even if they are only reading glasses required for looking at military analyses, maps, wire service copy, and typewriter keys. All of the dozen or so optometrists' shops in the central part of the city were shuttered, their owners safely overseas by now. Panic strikes different people in different ways and for me the panic set in when I began to believe I couldn't cover the war any more.

In desperation I asked a cyclo driver in front of the Caravelle, an entrepreneur who could get anybody anything, where I could get some new glasses and he shouted something in Vietnamese. We were suddenly surrounded by people trying to sell us glasses. They produced glasses from everywhere, from their pockets and hats and from beneath the cushions of their cyclos and taxis: horn rims, metal rims, and bifocals. Ti Ti the jasmine girl had about eight pairs which she produced from somewhere in her raggedy clothing and she started her sales pitch by calling me "gentleman" and ended with her usual, "You number ten cheap Charlie."

There was obviously a glut of glasses in the city and I felt better. In the circumstances I even became fussy. I told the cyclo driver I wanted a pair properly made for me by an optometrist. He shook his head at this madness but waved away the now angry horde of spectacle sellers and pedalled me to the central market.

He found an old man in the market who sat me on a stool in a gutter and sent an assistant across the alley to hold a card with letters on it. Then he fitted an array of lenses into metal frames over my eyes until I found I could read the card clearly, and he made me a pair of glasses that lasted for years. They cost the equivalent of $7.50, including the cyclo's exorbitant commission, and I felt the sort of relief that comes after safely crossing a minefield.

The Americans and other foreigners were pouring out of the city in these last weeks on the commercial airlines or the American evacuation flights making it lonely. The Canadian chargé d'affaires, Ernest Hébert, ordered all Canadians out on two final C-130s but he knew the newsmen wouldn't go. Cooperatively

113

he pulled down the flag on the Canadian Embassy a few times so the TV cameras could catch it.

Brian Ellis, the genial CBS bureau chief, now the network's foreign editor, organized an amazing evacuation of Vietnamese employees of the news services and their dependents, smuggling at least 1,200 of them to the planes at Tan Son Nhut airport in everything from cyclos to garbage trucks, with the tacit agreement of U.S. Ambassador Martin.

The demand for the Ellis evacuation service became so desperate he had to change hotels every night, from the Caravelle to the Continental to the Majestic, in order to escape the mobs who pounded on his doors. Some of his clients produced pistols and laid them casually on their laps as they tried to convince him of their present or previous connections with the networks.

We were all scared. The correspondent who is not scared in such circumstances is stupid. But a feeling of fatalism sets in. There is nothing at all you can do about the events around you except to follow the correspondent's edict and "take care" not to do anything rash. And this feeling of fatalism is mixed with the exhilaration of being on the big story and the joy of the company of friends who are among the best professionals in the business.

There was only one decision to make: whether to stay after the fall or get out, because it was still possible to get out almost to the end, on flights sent to evacuate the embassy staffs who were leaving in droves, the Australians, the Canadians, the Taiwanese, the British, until only the French and Americans remained. I even went home to Hong Kong and back on a commercial flight on April 21 to pick up some money.

Some correspondents were ordered home by their offices, sometimes because of the danger and sometimes the expense. It was costing *The Toronto Star* over $10,000 a month in insurance premiums alone for their one man on the scene. Insurance was triple that for a TV crew. Some correspondents and crews went of their own accord. One Radio Canada crew flew in in the last days and asked my advice, as the senior Canadian correspondent in the area, about the situation. They seemed surprised that there was a real war going on a few miles away with bullets and bombs.

"It does not seem to be civilized here," the Québecois correspondent remarked at the end of my briefing. He and his crew stayed for about two days, interviewed the Archbishop of Saigon, and took off hurriedly for home.

Peter Hazlehurst of *The Times* and I talked over our options and made our decisions over cups of lemon tea in the Tu Do Street restaurant a week or so before the fall. Hazelhurst is a gentle man who used to be a stunt pilot in an air circus in his native South Africa. He was spending much of his time trying to "save" the girls in the Miramar Hotel, listening to their stories for hours on end, telling them they'd be all right if only they would go home to the families they were supporting. But he was scared too and we talked of our mutual fears over the cups of tea.

We had both asked the senior members of the Viet Cong delegation to the International Control Commission, which held press conferences regularly every Saturday at their headquarters at Tan Son Nhut, whether correspondents would be killed after "liberation" and they'd vaguely assured us they would not. But we didn't believe it. Both of us, wrongly as it turned out, predicted a bloodbath when the Communists marched into Saigon.

We decided that because we were one-man bureaus it would be professionally senseless to stay after "liberation" because there was unlikely to be any means of communication with our home countries and we would be unable to file the story of the last hours and whatever followed. Better, we decided, to go with the evacuation of the last of the Americans, providing an evacuation occurred and that the Americans would take a Brit and a Canadian with them, because the evacuation would be the big story and we could file it from wherever it took us. But it was a decision based as much on personal fear as it was on professionalism.

Most of the time, though, we were too busy to contemplate our personal feelings for long.

It was impossible for an individual newsman to keep up with the events, military and political, in the last few weeks. A huge C-5A transport carrying 257 orphans to America crashed soon after take off from Tan Son Nhut on April 4, killing 155 people. I was "down the road" at the time and I heard about it from the BBC in London on my little shortwave radio. I covered myself by cabling the office and suggesting they take the wire service stories, thus letting them know that I was at least aware of the incident.

A lone plane flown by a South Vietnamese defector swooped twice over the city on April 8, bombing the presidential palace on the second run, killing two palace guards. I ran through the pandemonium of startled troops and scurrying civilians to file the story at the Reuters office, a few hundred yards from the palace, then prepared to hole up there, near the communications system, for the "liberation" we expected to follow. But it didn't come then. A twenty-four hour curfew was soon lifted and I walked through the empty streets back to the hotel.

The huge Bien Hua ammunition dump exploded in the early morning hours of April 15. It was about twenty-five miles away but it shook the city and tumbled me out of bed.

Refugees from the north poured by ship and barge into Vung Tau, the seaside resort south of Saigon, providing pathetic interviews when you could reach them along a road cut in several places by the Communists. One large family I interviewed had fled from Hue to Da Nang and then to Nha Trang before finally making it to Vung Tau in a barge. They said the mother of the family had slipped and fallen during the voyage from Nha Trang and died from her injuries and exhaustion.

The family was carrying four little bundles wrapped in green military cloth and I asked the eldest son what was in them.

"These three are rice and clothes," he said. "That one there is mother."

Xuan Loc, on Highway 1, about thirty-five miles north of Saigon fell finally on April 21 after being bravely defended by the Vietnamese Eighteenth Division. It was the last stand and the Americans tried their final desperate trick there.

They imported a secret CBU55 bomb, never used before or since, from storage in Thailand and had a Vietnamese Air Force C-130 drop it on the little city during the last days of its defense. Its secret combination of chemicals was designed to burn oxygen at such a rate it literally sucked the air from the lungs of anyone within a quarter of a mile of where it hit. It killed about 250 North Vietnamese troops, leaving their bodies oddly intact. Reconnaissance pictures showed fixed expressions of wide-eyed horror on the faces of the dead. But it didn't stop the Communist advance.

Nguyen Van Thieu finally resigned as president on April 21 to be replaced by Vice President Tran Van Huong and then by Duong Van Minh (Big Minh) but that didn't stop the advance either.

Thieu's wife, rich from corruption already, owner of a villa in Switzerland, tried to send sixteen tons of the country's gold on a chartered Swiss airline, but the pilots, for safety reasons, demanded to know the contents of the boxes. They conferred with the Swiss consulate, then refused to fly out the fortune.

Instead, then, she had corrupt officials find her a ship which took the gold and piles of diamonds and jade to France. She also took many antiques, mostly belonging to the government, although unknown to her many of them had been replaced with worthless replicas by corrupt museum officials.

Mrs. Thieu asked her husband's military aide, General Dang Van Quang, to look after the antiques for her. Quang is a very fat man whom we used to call "Giggles." He made most of his fortune in the heroin trade while his wife ran brothels in the Mekong Delta. Quang had the genuine antiques and the copies from the museum loaded on a ship that traveled via the U.S. to Montreal, where he now lives. Mrs. Thieu supervised the packing personally.

Then the Thieus themselves left for Taiwan in the early morning hours of April 26, on a super secret flight by a U.S. C-118 aircraft. They carried four suitcases stuffed with dollar bills in big denominations.

I was in the antique business myself in these last days. The day before the Thieus fled, Tony Paul insisted on buying a present for his wife for their wedding anniversary on May 2 and he asked for my help. I took him to the classiest antique store in the city, on the first floor of the building across from the Caravelle Hotel, where the best of the Vietnamese antiques had been sold honestly though expensively throughout the war.

It was still stocked with beautiful Ming bowls and vases, most of them so big they couldn't be carried away, and with finely carved silverware and pieces of jade, but there were no customers anymore, just the two saleswomen who had served with silent dignity a generation of the city's richer and more discriminating locals and visitors.

Paul's eyes lit on a strange looking apparatus, a water pipe, with an elaborately carved ivory bowl and a thin bamboo stem curving about two feet above it. It was a big ugly thing but it fascinated him. He figured he would be able to get it out of the country somehow and he bought it for a hundred dollars.

I was looking at the jade pieces, mainly because they were small and smugglable, but I couldn't make up my mind so I asked the senior saleswoman to point out the most expensive piece of jade they had in the store.

She looked through her catalogue and pointed to two delicate, small bowls and saucers, with lids.

"How much?" I asked.

"A million piastres," she said.

I am just not used to dealing in millions of any sort of money, even piastres which were then losing their value by about fifty percent a day.

"I'll give you $120 for them," I said.

"OK," she said, without even a smile. And she wrapped them for me in two little boxes.

Malcolm Gray, of the Toronto *Globe and Mail*, had been ordered to leave Saigon that day and he agreed to smuggle the jade pieces out for me and deliver them to Marie in Hong Kong.

"Be very careful," I warned him. "They're worth at least a million piastres."

He treated them with great care, bribing the customs at Tan Son Nhut much more than the usual amount and hugging them on his lap all the way to Hong Kong.

When I got home myself much later I suggested to Marie that we should take the jade pieces to Mr. Wong, our jeweler, for a valuation.

Mr. Wong examined the pieces carefully.

119

"Quite nice pieces of new jade," he said eventually. "Better than some we get in Hong Kong. Worth at least a hundred dollars, maybe even a hundred and twenty."

I walked casually into the Reuters office to file a story on the morning of April 28. Pat Massey, the wire service's chief reporter, was running to the door knocking some files to the floor in his rush.

"Do you have a car?" he yelled at me. "I need a car straight away."

"I've got a car," I said, "but what the hell is all the rush about?"

He led me into the street outside the dingy little office and held a hand to an ear. "Listen," he instructed.

Very vaguely in the distance I could hear the crump, crump sounds of a rocket or artillery barrage.

"They've arrived," Massey announced. "It's over."

We climbed in the car and told the driver to go toward the direction of the sounds. He was a driver I had not known until I hired him just for the short run to the Reuters office and he did not want to go to the war. We had to abuse him and offer him more money.

At the Newport Bridge, just three miles from the center of Saigon, on the main highway leading to Bien Hua, South Vietnamese helicopter gunships were swooping low and firing rockets that whooshed and roared before they exploded on the banks of the narrow, dirty Dong Nai River.

A CBC TV crew, Peter Kent, Colin Hoath, Ian Wilson, and their producer George James, were standing in an open Jeep near the bridge entrance shouting at me.

"Don't go," Kent was shouting. "It's rough out there."

They had been trapped on the bridge with an NBC crew and some other newsmen in crossfire between defending ARVN soldiers and a small group of Viet Cong commandos firing mortars and machine guns at them. But Ian Wilson, the tough little CBC cameraman was laughing.

"Damndest thing I ever experienced," he said. "There were these heavy machine gun bursts and the bullets were whistling over our heads so we all threw ourselves flat on the deck of the bridge and began crawling beneath the bullets on our stomachs, except for Hilary Brown, [the tall NBC correspondent] who moved along on her hands and knees. Maybe she didn't want to get her bush jacket dirty. And everybody was shouting, 'For Christ's sake get your arse down Hilary.' Somehow it seemed funny, seeing Hilary, arse up in the air, and with all the shouting at her, and we all burst out laughing. It was a strange time and place to be laughing."

Massey and I walked separately to the bridge entrance. The helicopter gunships were still bombarding the river banks making a terrible noise, and the sixty-odd Communist commandos who had slipped into the city had set fire to a fuel dump on the right bank of the river, covering everything with big belches of smoke. There was a deserted roadside stall, the Thanh Huan Café, near the bridge entrance and I sat on one of its stools and helped myself to some still warm noodles while I watched the last real battle of the thirty-year war.

The ARVN soldiers on the bridge fought bravely, standing up at times in the hail of bullets to get a better shot back. Ambulances pulled up near my little restaurant viewpoint to carry the wounded away. It was impossible to tell who was winning.

The car had gone when I came off the bridge and I had deadlines in Toronto so I ran about half a mile through streets and markets that seemed amazingly quiet and normal. A man on a Honda took pity on me and offered a lift on his pillion to the Reuters office. Then I slept through the rest of the start of the end. My deadlines for that day had passed anyway.

Four captured South Vietnamese Air Force A-37s dropped a dozen 500-pound bombs on the military area at Tan Son Nhut air base about six that evening and the city errupted simultaneously with small arms fire, from Communist infiltrators, South Vietnamese soldiers, police and civilians. Just about everybody, I was told, started firing guns in the streets of Saigon, especially in Lam Son Square just outside my third-storey hotel window, in order to create panic or because of it.

And everybody, with the possible exceptions of U.S. Ambassador Martin and me, knew that finally it was indeed all over. Martin was refusing to chop down the big tree in the courtyard of the U.S. embassy so that helicopters could land for an evacuation everybody else knew was now urgent.

Others told me the story of the eruption in the city. Tony Paul was having a drink on the patio of the Continental Palace Hotel, on the other side of the square from my room, when the bombing and shooting started. Bullets whistled above his head as he scattered chairs and tables to throw himself on the floor.

Colin Hoath, the CBC correspondent, was just about to sign off his circuit to Toronto when all hell broke loose outside and he thought the old broadcasting building was under attack. He kept his circuit open for a good live story.

John Pilger, of the London *Daily Mirror*, was conducting a black-market money exchange at the Indian tailor shop on Tu Do Street.

"You are most fortunate," the Indian told him calmly as bullets whined around them. "Thanks to the gentlemen who have just bombed us, the rate has risen a thousand piastres—but only hundred dollar bills please."

But I was taking an unusual early evening nap and none of it disturbed me. It had been a tough day, a fairly tough month.

The big barrage hit Tan Son Nhut airport just before dawn on April 29 and woke everybody up, even me.

I had interrupted my nap of the evening before when the first bombs fell and the city erupted in gunfire, to have dinner and attend a correspondents' meeting in the Caravelle's rooftop bar where we were supposed to hear about plans for our evacuation, if an evacuation was ever called.

The meeting was vague and inconclusive. The signal would be a statement on the American FM station that the temperature was 112 degrees and rising, followed by the playing of "White Christmas," presumably the Bing Crosby version. Then we were to go to 3 Phan Van Dat Street, a block east of Tu Do, near the Saigon River, and wait. But the U.S. embassy was obviously still in confusion. Ambassador Martin was still refusing to cut down the damn tree and there was no indication of when, or even if, an evacuation would occur. So I switched on the radio in my room to listen for "White Christmas" and went back to sleep.

Everybody rushed to the roof of the Caravelle when the barrage hit, the TV crews crushing their cameras and equipment into the small elevators. The air base a few miles away was aflame. Columns of black smoke rose and spread and covered it like a low cloud. The whole city rumbled with the noise and just after dawn a twin-tailed flying boxcar, hit by a SAM missile, caught fire slowly and circled down and down like a plane in a slow motion movie.

I filed my story about 9 A.M., picking up the news

at Reuters that two American marines had been killed in the continuing attack and that Ambassador Martin was on his way to the airport and was likely now, at last, to order an evacuation. I added a note stating this would probably be my last file out of Saigon. If an evacuation occurred I was going with it.

But the copy moved slowly and I stayed in the Reuters office for a while, waiting for any more news from the U.S. Embassy, so it was about noon before I walked through empty streets back to the hotel.

Almost everybody had gone. There were a few correspondents in the lobby, looking anxious, and I asked Hilary Brown what was going on.

"They've pulled the plug," she said. "Only one chance to leave—now! Aren't you going?"

I was going. I packed my bags in a bit of a hurry, left a pile of piastres for the room boys, paid my bill, and began to walk alone toward the pick up point on Phan Van Dat Street. The jasmine girl outside the Caravelle, who might have been Ti Ti's older sister, tried to sell me a string of flowers and called me, "Cheap Charlie." Then she seemed to suddenly relent in her rudeness. "Bye bye Canada," she said quietly. "Take care."

There was absolutely nobody on Tu Do Street and nobody at either the pick up point in front of a multi-storey apartment building formerly occupied by American families. The building itself was also ominously empty.

I discovered later the departure point had been changed at the last minute because the South Vietnamese Navy had placed a machine gun on the roof of the building. U.S. Embassy officials had some doubts about whether the sailors planned to fire on Communists or on U.S. evacuation helicopters.

I waited for about half an hour, feeling very lonely. Then a car carrying three other correspondents arrived and they bundled me in with them to drive to another assembly point they knew about—a hospital, four blocks north.

A crowd of about 300 had gathered near this building under a faded sign: University of Maryland, Saigon Education Centre. It was hot and the inevitable street vendors were selling cold beer.

Then three ancient, gray buses arrived and we surged onto them, those of us who could fit, packed together so we could hardly move, sweating, as the one I squeezed into took a circuitous two-hour route to the airport.

A plane spiraled down from the sky and crashed somewhere in the Cholon area of the city as we neared the airport and there was the sound of small arms fire after we passed through the gates, apparently from South Vietnamese guards who refused to allow a following bus to enter. The airport was still under artillery fire and huts and vehicles were wrecked and smoldering from the earlier attacks. A 130 mm shell hit the tarmac a few hundred feet from the bus, with a terrifying explosion, just as we stopped at the Pentagon East, the U.S. millitary headquarters at Tan Son Nhut.

Peter Collins, the CBS correspondent, had his Vietnamese wife and family with him. "Oh my God," he said. "Not here, not now."

Tony Paul was on the seat behind me. He was rescuing his Vietnamese interpreter and his family and was carrying several small children on his knees and a bag in which he had carefully packed his ugly antique water pipe. He was also clutching a brand-new ARVN lieutenant-general's cap, its peak impressively encrusted with gold-braided laurel leaves, which he had bought the day before for a souvenir. ARVN general's caps were going quite cheaply.

Later, when an order came to dump all luggage before boarding an evacuation helicopter, Paul refused to surrender his precious water pipe and he saved his general's cap by simply placing it on his head.

The heavy metal ramp of the big chopper he ran to was just being lowered as he tried to help some of his interpreter's children on board and it settled on the toe of one of his shoes, missing by millimeters crushing his toes. But his shoe was trapped and he couldn't move while refugees surged up the ramp past him. A Frenchwoman tried to help him drag his foot free, but it didn't work and in the end he had to abandon the shoe on the ground.

"I dropped from the chopper onto the flight deck of the *Midway* and lined up for processing by the marines," he told me later. "When it was my turn to give my name and particulars, the marine clerk looked up from his pad, taking in this large bush-jacketed man wearing a gold-braided general's cap and one shoe and holding aloft an antique ivory water pipe with its great bamboo stem waving in the air. A look of infinite disgust formed on his face.

" 'Aw, fercrissake,' the marine demanded of no one in particular. 'Who the fuck are they sending us *now*?' "

Keyes Beech, the veteran Asian correspondent for the Chicago *Daily News*, one of the best of the old hands, was in one of the other buses. He filed this report:

We heard the bad news on the driver's radio on the way out: "Security conditions are out of control at Tan Son Nhut. Do not go to Tan Son Nhut. Repeat, do not go to Tan Son Nhut." . . . It was 2 P.M. when we headed back to the city. Nobody on that bus will ever forget the next few hours . . .

At every stop Vietnamese beat on the doors and windows pleading to be let inside. We merely looked at them . . . Every time we opened the door we had to beat and kick them back.

For no reason except that we were following another bus we went to the Saigon port area, one of the toughest parts of the city, where the crowds were uglier than elsewhere . . .

I got off the bus and went over to John Moore, the embassy security officer, who was sitting in one of those sedans with the flashy blinkers on the top. "Do you know why we are here and what you are going to do with us?" I asked him. Moore shrugged helplessly. "There are ships," he said, gesturing toward sand-bagged Vietnamese vessels lying alongside the dock. I looked around at the gathering crowd. Small boys were snatching typewriters and bags of film. This, as the Chinese would say, looked like a bad joss. I didn't know how or whether I was going to get out of Saigon, but I damn well knew I wasn't going to stay here. I got back on the bus . . . I found myself pushing a middle-aged Vietnamese woman who had been sitting beside me and had asked me to look after her because she worked for the Americans and the Vietcong would cut her throat. That's what they all said, and maybe they are right. But she fought her way back to my side. "Why did you push me?" she asked. I had no answer.

Austin, the driver, didn't know what to do with us so we drove to the American Embassy. There the Viet-namese women decided to get off. "I have worked for the United States Government for ten years," she said, "but you do not trust me and I do not trust you. Even if we do get to Tan Son Nhut, they wouldn't let me on a plane." She was right, of course. "I am going home to poison myself," she said. I didn't say anything because there was nothing to say.

There was only one way inside the embassy—through the crowd and over the ten-foot wall. Once we moved into that seething mass we ceased to be correspondents. We were only men fighting for our lives, scratching, clawing, pushing even closer to that wall . . . We were like animals. Now, I thought, I know what it's like to be a Vietnamese. I am one of them. But if I could get over the wall I would be an American again.

Somebody grabbed my sleeve and wouldn't let go. I turned my head and looked into the face of a Vietnamese youth. "You adopt me and take me with you and I'll help you," he screamed. "If you don't, you don't go." I said I'd adopt him. I'd have said anything. Could this be happening to me? Suddenly my arm was free, and I edged closer to the wall. There was a pair of Marines on the wall. They were trying to help us and kick the Vietnamese down. One of them looked down at me. "Help me," I pleaded. "Please help me."

That Marine helped me. He reached down with his long, muscular arm and pulled me up as if I was a helpless child. I lay on a tin roof gasping for breath like a landed fish . . . God bless the Marines. I was one myself in the last of the just wars. One American offered me a cup of water and a doctor asked me if I wanted a tranquilizer. I accepted the water and declined the tranquilizer.

Hong Kong

The bile from this python was put into my wine — guaranteed to keep the drinker warm all winter!

Thousands of people live on the water in Aberdeen, Hong Kong.

This is the widest street in the walled city of Kowloon. Most of these businesses are dentists and denture sellers.

Minutes after a rocket attack on Phnom Penh the newsmen are on the spot, risking a second attack. On the left is Neil Davis (see chapter 8), on the right Jon Swain of the *Sunday Times*.

Millions of Cambodians fled the Khmer Rouge genocide. I photographed this child in 1976, in a refugee camp in Thailand.

The night before Da Nang fell to the Viet Cong forces on March 28, 1975, its population was doubled by the influx of refugees from the fighting farther north

Refugees waiting on the dockside at Da Nang

329BZM V
      R I
        AM-WITNESS 3-29-
        FLIGHT FROM DA NANG
        A PERSONAL REPORT
        BY PAUL VOGLE
        DA NANG, VIETNAM, MARCH 29 (UPI) -- ONLY THE FASTEST, THE STRONGEST, AND THE MEANEST OF A HUGE MOB GOT A RIDE ON THE LAST PLANE FROM DA NANG SATURDAY.
        PEOPLE DIED TRYING TO GET ABOARD AND OTHERS DIED WHEN THEY FELL THOUSANDS OF FEET INTO THE SEA BECAUSE EVEN DESPERATION COULD NO LONGER KEEP THEIR FINGERS WELDED TO THE UNDERCARRIAGE.
        IT WAS A FLIGHT INTO HELL, AND ONLY A GOOD, TOUGH AMERICAN PILOT AND A LOT OF PRAYERS GOT US BACK TO TAN SON NHUT AIR BASE ALIVE -- WITH THE BOEING 727 FLAPS JAMMED AND THE WHEELS FULLY EXTENDED.
        IT WAS A RIDE I'LL NEVER FORGET.
        WORLD AIRWAYS PRESIDENT ED DALY WAS ABOARD. HE WAS ANGRY AND TIRED. DALY SAID HE HAD BEEN UP ALL NIGHT ARGUING WITH AMERICAN AND VIETNAMESE OFFICIALS FOR PERMISSION TO FLY INTO BESEIGED DA NANG TO GET SOME MORE REFUGEES OUT.
        DALY FINALLY SAID TO HELL WITH PAPERWORK, CLEARANCES, AND CAUTION AND WE WERE ON OUR WAY.
        IT SEEMED PEACEFUL ENOUGH AS WE TOUCHED DOWN AT THE AIRPORT 370 MILES NORTHEAST OF SAIGON.
        OVER A THOUSAND PEOPLE HAD BEEN WAITING AROUND A QUONSET HUT SEVERAL HUNDRED YARDS AWAY FROM WHERE WE TOUCHED DOWN.
        SUDDENLY IT WAS A MOB IN MOTION. THEY ROARED ACROSS THE TARMAC ON MOTORBIKES, JEEPS, LAMBRETTA SCOOTERS, AND ON LEGS SPEEDED BY SHEER DESPERATION AND PANIC.
        ED DALY AND I STOOD NEAR THE BOTTOM OF THE 727'S TAIL RAMP. DALY HELD OUT HIS ARMS WHILE I SHOUTED IN VIETNAMESE, "ONE AT A TIME, ONE AT A TIME. THERE'S ROOM FOR EVERYBODY."
        THERE WASN'T ROOM FOR EVERYBODY AND EVERYBODY KNEW DAMN WELL THERE WASN'T.
        DALY AND I WERE KNOCKED ASIDE AND BACKWARD.
        IF ED DALY THOUGHT HE'D GET SOME WOMEN AND CHILDREN OUT OF DA NANG HE WAS WRONG. THE PLANE WAS JAMMED IN AN INSTANT WITH TROOPS OF THE 1ST DIVISION'S MEANEST UNIT, THE JAC BAO (BLACK PANTHERS).
        THEY LITERALLY RIPPED THE CLOTHES RIGHT OFF DALY ALONG WITH SOME OF HIS SKIN. I SAW ONE OF THEM KICK AN OLD WOMAN IN THE FACE TO GET ABOARD.
        IN THE MOVIES SOMEBODY WOULD HAVE SHOT THE BASTARD AND HELPED THE OLD LADY ON THE PLANE. THIS WAS NO MOVIE. THE BASTARD FLEW AND THE OLD LADY WAS TUMBLING DOWN THE TARMAC, HER FINGERS CLAWING TOWARD A PLANE THAT WAS ALREADY ROLLING.

        A BRITISH CAMERAMAN WHO FLEW UP WITH US MADE THE MISTAKE OF GETTING OFF THE PLANE WHEN WE LANDED, TO SHOOT THE LOADING.
        HE COULD NOT GET BACK ABOARD IN THE PANDEMONIUM. IN THE VERY BEST TRADITION OF THE BUSINESS HE THREW HIS CAMERA WITH ITS PRECIOUS FILM INTO THE CLOSING DOOR AND STOOD THERE AND WATCHED THE PLANE TAKE OFF ...
        AS WE STARTED ROLLING, INSANITY GRIPPED THOSE WHO HAD MISSED THE LAST CHANCE. GOVERNMENT TROOPS OPENED FIRE ON US. SOMEBODY LOBBED A HAND GRENADE TOWARDS THE WING. THE EXPLOSION JAMMED THE FLAPS FULL OPEN AND THE UNDERCARRIAGE AT FULL EXTENSION.
        COMMUNIST ROCKETS BEGAN EXPLODING AT A DISTANCE.
        OUR PILOT, KEN HEALY, 52, OF OAKLAND, CALIF., SLAMMED THE THROTTLES OPEN AND LURCHED INTO THE AIR FROM THE TAXIWAY. THERE WAS NO WAY WE COULD HAVE SURVIVED THE GUNFIRE AND GOT INTO THE MAIN RUNWAY.
        A BACKUP 727 HAD FLOWN BEHIND US BUT HAD BEEN ORDERED NOT TO LAND WHEN THE PANIC BROKE OUT. IT'S PILOT RADIOED THAT HE COULD SEE THE LEGS OF PEOPLE HANGING DOWN FROM THE UNDERCARRIAGE OF OUR PLANE.
        UPI PHOTOGRAPHER LIEN HUONG, WHO WAS IN THE COCKPIT OF THAT BACKUP PLANE, SAW AT LEAST ONE PERSON LOSE HIS GRIP ON LIFE AND PLUMMET INTO THE SOUTH CHINA SEA BELOW.
        MORE
        UPI 03-26 03:37 PED

A piece of copy fresh from the wire machine, courtesy of United Press International

Refugees on the trail of tears near Xuan Loc, traveling south to Saigon

These Vietnamese refugees had managed to travel by boat from Da Nang to Vung Tau. The bundle the young man is carrying contains his mother who died on the journey.

On board the *U.S.S. Sergeant Miller*. The leg belongs to Mike Sullivan of the BBC.

The round eye family on board the *Sergeant Miller* took turns to rest under the sun shade

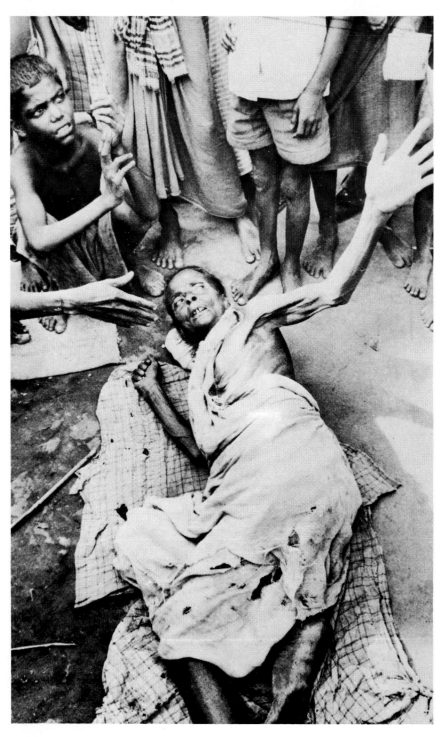

In Dacca, Bangladesh, people die of starvation on the street

# CHAPTER 8

# The last of the bush jackets

On April 28, the day before I arrived at the Pentagon East for evacuation, Neil Davis, the blond, baby-faced Australian freelance TV cameraman, strolled down Tu Do Street with Rick Herron, the longtime AP photographer in Vietnam, pushing their way through the girls and the money changers until they came to the little shop, on the left side of the street, halfway between the Continental and Caravelle Hotels and the Saigon River. The shop sign said "Minh the Tailor."

Minh was the first tailor to design and make the correspondents' suit, with its buttoned jacket pockets and the slots in the sleeves to take pens and a notebook. He made his first bush jacket back in 1962, before anybody knew or cared much about the Vietnam war. He had a thousand imitators all over Saigon, and later all over Asia and the world, but still nobody, it was generally believed among correspondents, made a bush jacket of the quality, style and fit of a genuine Mr. Minh.

Davis had fled from Phnom Penh, five days before it fell to the cruel Khmer Rouge on April 17. He was the senior correspondent in Cambodia, a longtime resident, and he knew from his experience and his intuition that the gentle land he loved was about to become a bloodbath.

He had had to abandon, in his flight from Phnom Penh, all of his possessions, a household of furniture and valuable artifacts, his car and his clothing, so that he had only the one suit he escaped in. And now, with Saigon collapsing around him, Davis was determined to restart his wardrobe with a genuine Mr. Minh.

Merron told him he was crazy and laughed at him. It was well known that Mr. Minh took at least forty-eight hours to make a suit, and Saigon didn't have that much time left. But Davis persisted.

Minh himself had gone by then, eventually to open a tailor shop in the United States, but he had left his head tailor in charge. Davis took a long time to pick the material for a cream-colored suit and to haggle with the head tailor over the price of it until they eventually agreed on the equivalent of five dollars.

Merron thought the whole thing was hilarious.

"I can't believe it," he told Davis. "You're into an *On The Beach* mentality. You're nuts. You'll never pick up your suit."

And next day when Merron, one of the best and bravest of the war photographers, saw Davis standing in a Saigon street as the evacuation bus carried him and me and other correspondents to what we hoped was safety, he still couldn't contain his mirth.

"Davis can't come with us," Merron told everybody within hearing. "He's got to stay and pick up his suit from Mr. Minh's."

Davis was one of about thirty correspondents who stayed behind in Saigon, some by accident but most, bravely, on purpose. Most of them were French, British, or Japanese, but there were also a few Americans—running the biggest risks of all—including almost the entire staffs of the two major wire services, AP and UPI.

Neil Davis told me his story of the fall of Saigon five years later when he was based in Bangkok working for NBC.

Early on the morning of April 30 he went to the American Embassy. Somewhere between 10,000 and 20,000 Vietnamese—and a few foreigners—were besieging the place. It was about 7:30 A.M. and at a few minutes to eight the last U.S. Marine Corps helicopter landed on the roof of the embassy. Somehow the mob on the ground sensed that it was the last one and with a violent rush it forced the embassy gates open. Soon it had the doors open as well.

The mood of the crowd was not hostile although some were shouting Vietnamese obscenities to the American marines on the roof, who were throwing tear gas canisters down among them. Davis was swearing at the marines too, in Vietnamese. *"Do-Mai,"* he was shouting, which means "mother fucker."

But there was no real belligerence, more a spirit of camaraderie on the ground. People seemed to think it was a good lark and looting had never seemed such fun. Davis didn't see one argument about who flogged what. He was offered a good-looking shirt from some American's abandoned suitcase. It fitted him too. The marines had thrown several tear gas canisters down inside the building but it barely hindered the looting. People took the strangest things. Of course the air conditioners went and the telephones, some of them still ringing as they were torn from their connections. Everything vent, light fittings, desks, filing cabinets— the files were scattered all over the place—carpeting, chairs, anything that could possibly be moved. One ARVN soldier took the end of one of the fire hoses and marched solemnly down a passage with it. Davis didn't wait to see what happened when he finally unwound the hose to its full length and found the other end was built into the wall.

One item that didn't seem to be valued by anybody, however, was firearms. There were discarded M16 rifles and all kinds of pistols everywhere, left behind by looting ARVN soldiers and the fleeing Americans, but nobody gave a damn about them.

Davis went back to his Kombi-bus and found an ARVN soldier industriously removing the battery. As gently as possible he explained that he wanted to use the bus and it would be a problem without the battery. The man was a bit reluctant until Davis pointed out lots of other vehicles abandoned nearby and suggested that maybe there were batteries and probably radios and other goodies in them. The soldier finally agreed and left the van intact. Davis set off down Thon Nhut boulevard.

The Australian had waited eleven years for the biggest story of all—the fall of Saigon—and he wanted the most illustrative film of all. Then he realized he was sitting there looking at it—the president's palace.

He drove in the back way, which was wide open, and around to the front where the wide steps led to the main entrance hall. There was nobody there. The whole palace seemed empty. But then a young man in civilian clothes, whom Davis recognized as an office worker at the palace, ran down the steps.

"Do you want to see the president?" the man asked.

Davis just nodded and the man pointed back up the steps.

"He's on the first floor," the man said.

When Davis reached the top of the stairs he found himself face-to-face with Big Minh, who had been president then for forty-eight hours. He didn't recognize him for a moment. Big Minh was wearing a correspondent's suit. He was unshaven and his eyes were red from weeping. He had broadcast the surrender over the radio about an hour earlier.

Davis asked him what was happening and Minh replied simply: "The other side will be here shortly."

They talked for a few minutes and then Minh walked off down the long, wide hall, his head down. Davis took film as he went.

It was all like a dream, as if he was watching a movie plot unfold. He went downstairs and met old Mr. Huyen, the longtime president of the Senate and Big Minh's vice-president for those final hours, a good man he'd always liked because he had opposed Thieu constitutionally. Huyen embraced Davis warmly, then got into his little car. He said he was going home to be with his family.

By now the streets outside the palace were almost deserted. The people had wisely gone indoors to wait, although they didn't know what they were waiting for. Davis didn't know either. The only thing he felt relatively certain about was that if he survived the first minutes of a meeting with the Communists, he would be alive to film and tell the story.

On the palace grounds under some trees he saw about fifty ARVN soldiers, sitting quietly in the shade. There was an eerie quiet, not only in the palace but in the city itself. He walked over and saw that the soldiers were unarmed, their weapons neatly stacked in nearby military trucks. A captain walked over and started talking casually to Davis about the weather.

Then, along the street alongside the palace, Davis saw a tank approaching. Suddenly a tongue of red flame spurted from its cannon and then there was the noise of the shot.

"Jesus," Davis said to the captain, "what's that?"

"It's a Communist tank," the captain replied in what Davis describes as a ridiculously casual way.

"Come on," Davis said. "Is it a *coup d'état*?" He

still couldn't reconcile himself to the fact that a Viet Cong or North Vietnamese tank was in the heart of Saigon.

"It's a Communist tank," the captain repeated, casually as before.

Through a break in the trees Davis saw it wheeling around the corner into Cong Ly Street, which runs past the main wrought iron gates of the palace, and he recognized it, a Russian tank—low and sleek—with the number 843 on its side and the biggest Viet Cong flag he'd ever seen, held by a soldier sitting on the front.

Davis turned to the captain who was holding out his hand.

"Goodbye and good luck," the captain said.

Davis walked onto the broad lawn and put up his sound camera. This was it, the big story. Tank 843 smashed into the gates, tearing one side off its hinges and sending up a cloud of dust. The tank backed off and came again, making no mistake the second time. They were through.

The little soldier with the big flag jumped off the tank and ran toward the palace, and another Communist trooper headed toward Davis yelling. From thirty yards away, he kept the camera rolling on the tank barrelling toward the palace, but out of his left eye he could see the soldier—looking determined and aggressive—running right up to him, pointing a rifle.

"Just live another minute," Davis said to himself, "and you're home free."

The soldier was yelling and Davis put his hands up with the fifteen-pound camera held high in his right hand, and he let go with the greeting he'd practiced in Vietnamese:

"Welcome to Saigon, comrade," he said. "I've been waiting to film the liberation."

He though that ought to hold the soldier for just a second or two and it did.

Then the soldier said, belligerently, "You're an American." It was an accusation, not a question.

"No, no," Davis said. "I'm an Australian journalist." And then it suddenly struck him that if he knew much about the war and its participants, being an Australian wouldn't exactly make the Communist soldier burst into applause.

But it steadied him for those vital few seconds. He hesitated and his eyes shifted focus onto something happening behind Davis. The fifty-odd ARVN soldiers were surrendering. The Communist soldier waved the TV man away with a toss of his rifle and walked past. Davis' right arm was sore from holding the camera over his head and he let it down to his shoulder and started filming the surrender of the South Vietnamese troopers.

Then more tanks came, a whole column of them. Number 843 had outstripped them in the race for the palace, the symbol of the South Vietnamese regime, to go down forever in Vietnamese Communist history. The other tanks, about twenty of them, formed a semicircle facing the palace and groups of running infantrymen joined them.

By this time two soldiers, each carrying a Viet Cong flag, had made it to the first floor balcony and they started waving the flags furiously. Their comrades below raised rifles in the air and fired nonstop bursts and single rounds for about thirty seconds. But they'd forgotten one thing in their haste and in the sheer ecstasy of the moment. Thirty feet above the two Viet Cong flag wavers, stiff in the breeze, the South Vietnamese flag was still flying. It made one more great shot for the only correspondent to cover the very end of the war.

In the palace dozens of curious Communist troopers crowded around Big Minh, who had shown dignity and great courage during his two days in power and knew what he had to do in the end. He was treated correctly by the victors and taken away to make another broadcast.

The Communist soldiers were awe-struck as they wandered around the plush palace. They found Thieu's office and one sat down in the president's chair and put his feet up on the desk.

Davis found one shy, young trooper standing alone in the main hall. He looked a bit out of it, even homesick. He was maybe eighteen years old but looked younger and the cameraman offered his hand to him.

"Where are you from?" Davis asked the standard question.

"From Hanoi," the youngster said. That could have meant anywhere in North Vietnam.

Davis asked him his name and the young soldier hesitated many moments, obviously debating with himself whether he should reveal it. He seemed to be very shy about his name.

"My name," he said at last, "is Nguyen Van Thieu." He looked embarassed.

"It's quite a common name, you know," the young soldier explained.

Neil Davis went back to Mr. Minh's tailor shop on Tu Do Street several times in the next few days but it was closed, along with most of the other business establishments, as the owners waited to see what the new regime would do to them.

Then, about five days after the fall of the city, as he took an early-evening stroll, he saw that the little store was open again.

The head tailor explained that the authorities had declared that he must close Minh's shop because the owner had fled and nobody else would be allowed to operate the business.

"Your's is the only thing I have to finish," the tailor said. "There are two or three other orders but I'm sure the people have gone—and your's is the only correspondent's suit.

"Come back before five o'clock tomorrow, but not later than five, because they'll be along to close the shop then."

Davis went back next day at 4:45 P.M. The shop was just the same, full of its many materials and ready made shirts Minh always had ready for instant off-the-hook sales. The tailor finished wrapping the cream-colored suit just as the Communist K4 squad—the appropriations unit—marched to the door.

Five or six soldiers lined up outside the door in single file, rifles over their shoulders. The tailor turned out the lights and closed the door. Davis helped him pull the steel mesh grill across. Then the leader of the K4 squad put a lock on the grill and snapped it shut.

Mr. Minh's chief tailor walked off down Tu Do Street without a word, his head down.

And Davis turned up the street toward the old Continental Hotel, carrying under his arm the last of the genuine bush jackets.

CHAPTER 9

# The first of the boat people

There were hundreds of us, mostly Vietnamese who were better dressed than the average and seemed to be mainly government officials or employees of the U.S. embassy, packed into the narrow tunnels underneath the Pentagon East at Tan Son Nhut airport on April 29, 1975. The occasional noise of shells exploding outside was muffled and cheerful marines tried to organize us into groups ready to make a run for the helicopters.

At first they warned us we would be able to take only one small bag of possessions, and later they said we could take nothing at all. The Vietnamese, carrying all they now owned in the world, searched desperately through their bags, pulling out little things that would fit in a pocket. Skinny children suddenly became fat. The walls of the tunnel were lined with thrown-away radios, clothing, food, and here and there a few framed family photographs. I held onto an airline bag, just big enough to carry my typewriter, a spare camera lens, and a bottle of whisky, and I wore the Nikon by its shoulder strap. A marine captain inspected me and said: "You're OK, good luck."

Every few minutes a door opened far away at the end of the tunnel. Then the roar of a chopper could be heard beyond the voices of marines shouting, "Go, go, go," and the single-file queue moved a few paces along the tunnel wall.

The door opened at fairly regular intervals, like a shutter on a camera letting in a shaft of light and after one opening, I remarked, to myself I thought: "I suppose that's the light at the end of the tunnel." I didn't think it was all that funny, but the American journalists around me roared with laughter. And the little joke, recalling President Lyndon Johnson's famous phrase of optimism on Vietnam, spread among some of the Vietnamese, who began to giggle as they sat among their discarded possessions, pointing along the shaft and saying in English: "Look, the light at the end of the tunnel."

Finally they were shouting, "Go, go, go" at me and I ran through the door. Marines with submachine guns were lying prone behind sandbags and there were two Jolly Green Giants, their motors roaring and rotors turning, on some tennis courts maybe a hundred yards away. The marines, flown in for just this operation, were stiff faced, grim. They looked scared and I ran like hell for the choppers.

The choppers were spending only two or three minutes on the ground, just long enough to gorge a load of about sixty people streaming from the tunnel. The rear loading ramp of the one I ran for was moving up toward the closed position as I scrambled along it. Oddly, a young Vietnamese stood up and gave me his seat as if I was an old lady on a crowded bus. The man next to me shook hands and said he was the minister for the interior, but that was the end of the conversation as the awkward big bird roared off the ground, zig-zagging to avoid small arms fire.

At the front of the crowded cabin, a big marine with blond, curly hair swung a huge machine gun that looked like a Browning left over from World War II, but couldn't have been, down toward the ground, then up through the air space, occasionally stiffening and aiming as if he had seen something, but he didn't fire.

While we were still ascending, still zig-zagging, a red flare swooped from the ground, creating in me the cold fear that it was a heat-seeking SAM missile. Others saw it too and clutched their seats or their children. But it spluttered out somewhere far below. And in about twenty minutes we crossed the coastline and felt safe.

It was dusk now and there were gray silhouettes of battleships strung across the ocean and the lights of scores of Jolly Green Giants and smaller Hueys blinking in the skies. We landed on the afterdeck of the *Denver*, one of the bigger ships, just as a group of sailors was pushing a Huey with Vietnamese markings over the stern. Its motor was still hot and it sizzled. It was the tenth Vietnamese chopper, the sailors told us, they had pushed overboard that day after escaping soldiers and their families landed in them.

Other newsmen appeared on the deck, Bill Stewart of *Time* magazine, Hugh Greenway of the Washington *Post*, Mel Proffitt, of *Newsweek*, and a few others, and we were separated from the Vietnamese and taken to a companionway where a cheerful young lieutenant checked our passports, registered us aboard, and took away our whisky. Like all U.S. Navy ships, the helicopter carrier *Denver* was dry.

Sailors escorted us to a huge mess, poured us Cokes in big paper cups and chatted while we joined them for our first meal since the shell-shattered dawn at the Caravelle Hotel. It seemed to be long, long ago. But it was obvious that, as newsmen, we were to be given special treatment on the *Denver* and there was talk that we would soon be flown to the flagship, *Blue Ridge*, where the other journalists were and where, we were told, there was a special communications center for filing our stories.

In the meantime the cheerful young lieutenant who had checked us in told us we could send one short telegram to a relative in the United States stating that we were safe on the *Denver*. I told him I was a Canadian and didn't have any relatives in the United States. He said: "Shit. That's tough. But that's the rule. I can't do anything about it."

I sent a wire to the *Star*'s veteran correspondent in Washington, Val Sears, addressed to Valerie Sears, care of the National Press Building, asking him to tell everybody at home I was OK and that they would be hearing from me shortly. I told the sailor checking the wires that Valerie was my cousin. Tough, masculine Val got the message and passed it on to the Toronto office.

It was only a minor frustration. Life felt good on the *Denver*, and safe. A lieutenant commander from Naval Intelligence took us to a wardroom and debriefed us, eliciting everything we knew about the fall of Saigon, including troop movements in the previous weeks, which didn't seem to matter much at that stage. And the senior captain of the ship (there were two captains) made a nice little speech in the mess, welcoming aboard the distinguished members of the national press.

Twice we waited on the deck for choppers to take us to the *Blue Ridge* and our other colleagues, but when a Huey finally landed and the cheerful lieutenant started to bundle us aboard, the U.S. Navy pilot said he had completely lost count of the hours he had flown since dawn and was too tired to take anybody anywhere in safety. But as a consolation the lieutenant promised he would somehow arrange to sent 200 words of news copy from each of us to the *Blue Ridge* for transmission to the United States.

By now there were about ten of us in our group, including a CIA man named Bert, and we were packed into a little cabin deep in the bowels of the ship, with a bunk for each of us. The typewriters clacked and the stories were sent. We let Greenway file first because he was worried that the Washington *Post* would be beaten by *The New York Times*. And I took a stroll on the deck, high up among the gun turrets, alone. The sea was still full of ships, shadowy in the distance, with only a few dim lights, and the sky was still crowded with choppers, swooping to the decks, taking off almost immediately and heading back to the coast. The night was balmy. And it was peaceful.

We were all exhausted and we slept in the air-conditioned cabin, with our clothes and typewriters at the end of our bunks. A voice on an intercom disturbed us occasionally, repeating: "All third-country nationals report immediately to the check-in station in the mess."

The message didn't worry me at all. I was surrounded by my American colleagues, some of them old friends. I had just been debriefed by American intelligence and it had never occurred to me not to tell them everything I knew. I didn't think of myself as a third-country national, whatever that meant. And I slept.

In the early hours of the morning a sailor was shaking me awake.

"Are you Cahill?" he asked. "Are you a third-country national?"

"I'm Cahill," I said sleepily. "What the hell is a third-country national?"

142

"Get your stuff together," he said. "Report to the mess."

Bert, the CIA man, climbed down from his upper bunk and confronted the sailor, who was carrying a baton.

"This guy's the same as the rest of us, sailor," he said. "He's a Canadian journalist. He's been covering the war the same as the rest of us. He's with us."

"He's got to go up to the mess deck," the sailor said. "Third-country nationals have to get off the ship."

The other journalists were awake by now.

"Don't worry, Jack," somebody said. "It will just be some administrative bullshit. If they try to kick you off, we'll stop them." I believe they tried.

Bert got dressed and came to the mess with the sailor and me. The young lieutenant, our guardian, wasn't cheerful any more. "I'm sorry," he said. "Gees, I'm sorry. The ship is going to the Philippines. And the Philippines government has said it will not accept any third-country nationals. So you're going to have to be put off the ship. But some other ship will pick you up and take you somewhere else, maybe Guam. It will be all right. Gees, I really am sorry," he said. There was no doubt he was sorry.

"Oh, for Christ's sake," I said. "The Philippines government just doesn't want the country flooded with Vietnamese refugees. They don't mean they won't let a Canadian journalist pass through. I'm a Canadian citizen. I've got my passport. I can go to the Philippines as a goddamn tourist without a visa even."

"It's the captain's orders," the lieutenant said.

"We want to see the captain," Bert the CIA man insisted, and eventually the junior of the captains came.

"I'm sorry," he said. "It's an order from Washington."

"But you're over-interpreting the bloody order," I said. "In these circumstances a third-country national means a Vietnamese refugee. I work with words, captain. I know what words mean. You can't always interpret them exactly. Have you checked with the other ships to see if they're kicking journalists off?"

"We've checked," he assured me. "Our senior captain says you're a third-country national and you've got to go."

"These bastards are crazy," Bert said. "The captain's gone round the bend. I'll see what I can do." He went away.

I was so tired I didn't care much any more.

The American sailors packed maybe 200 of us onto the landing barge in the bowels of the *U.S.S. Denver* and then flooded the hold slowly until we floated. Then the doors at the stern of the ship opened with a roar and a hiss and we were suddenly out in the open sea. The doors of the big, safe ship closed again and it floated away like a great swimming gray elephant that had just had a difficult bowel movement but had finally cleansed itself of us nonAmericans.

Except for me and a tall youngish man with fair skin and snow-white hair there seemed to be only Vietnamese on the barge and most of them looked dazed and bewildered. They had thought they had made it to safety at last on the *Denver*, as I had, and they were probably not even aware of the Captain's interpretation of the order that no "third country nationals" were to be taken on navy ships to the Philippines.

The sea was rough and the barge pitched and rolled, throwing people about. Some mothers tried to feed their children with a ration of rice the navy had given them, but it didn't work. Some of the children were seasick. Some spat out the food and cried. Some just stared at the lights from the Jolly Green Giants, still flickering in the dark sky, as they carried the last of the refugees from Saigon to big ships that we hoped would be more hospitable than the *Denver*.

The man with the white hair waved and began to move toward me, clutching the gunwale for support, and I moved toward him, trying not to slip on spilled rice or vomit or tread on children curled on the deck around the feet of their parents.

"I'm Mike Sullivan of the BBC," Sullivan said when we managed to get close enough to talk. "You a journalist?"

"Jack Cahill, *Toronto Star*," I said. We tried to shake hands but couldn't touch in the crush. "Nice to meet another third-country national."

"Crazy chaps, those Americans," Sullivan said.

We could see a few small lights at sea level in the distance and the sailor in charge of the barge steered us toward them through the big sloppy waves until the gray shape of a small ship became suddenly clear in the darkness. I had seen her before—the *U.S.S. Sgt. Andrew Miller*, veteran of the exodus from Da Nang, in which forty-three of its 10,000 refugee passengers died in two days. She was about 7,000 tons, manned by a civilian crew and a company of U.S. Marines.

We had to jump from the barge to a pontoon and then climb a ladder to get aboard the *Sgt. Miller* but the women and children all made it with the help of the men who then went back to the barge for the pathetic little packages that were their only possessions.

Sullivan's white hair must have been like a beacon to the tough sailors watching the scramble aboard and a few of them approached us as we stood on the deck wondering where to go and what to do next.

"Hell," one of them said, "what are you guys doing on a ship like this? We've got no water. We've got no food. We've got no shithouses, all we've got is bloody people." He pointed at the mass of Vietnamese around us and indicated that he regarded us as different. Then he added: "This is a cargo ship, you know. We're not set up for people of any sort. But good luck. Now move on."

A notice near the top of the gangway said in Vietnamese and English: "Don't spit on the deck. Don't urinate on the deck. Don't defecate on the deck. Keep calm."

A marine with an automatic rifle hustled Sullivan and me with a group of other refugees to the bow of the ship and we sat on the steel deck, tired and quiet, and we slept a little until it began to rain heavily. There were about 2,000 refugees on the ship then and we thought it was packed tight, but somehow they crammed in at least another 5,000 in the next twenty-four hours.

We were soaked by the rain so we climbed down into a hold but it was packed with people and the family we lay among had a crippled child who was also retarded and he made sleep difficult. So we climbed down even farther into the lowest hold in the ship and found some fairly dry space among some Vietnamese helicopter pilots who had flown their families in the choppers to the U.S. fleet as Saigon fell.

The hold stank. Kids were crapping in one corner. The chopper pilots made room on the deck among their families and loaned us their army bags for pillows and plastic bags to spread on the wet rusty metal and we had our first sleep since the rocket attack on Saigon more than twenty-four hours before.

Saigon fell at noon that day and all day long barges, sampans, fishing boats and fair-sized ships packed with people hovered around the *Sgt. Miller*, but the marines kept most of them away by firing into the water nearby.

Still the ship, apparently under orders from

146

Washington to pick up as many refugees as possible, moved closer to the coast near the refugee center of Vung Tau, until it was well within Vietnamese territorial waters and the coast was clearly visible.

At about one P.M., deep down in the ship, we heard booming noises and a marine shouted: "We're under fire." We climbed up the ladders to the deck and there were shells exploding in the water a few hundred yards from the stern. We could see the flashes from the shore batteries and the splashes near the ship, but we must have been just out of range because they always fell about the same distance behind as we moved out to sea.

As soon as the firing began a destroyer and a helicopter carrier escorting us sped off to sea as if officialdom wanted to have nothing at all to do with whatever we were doing.

We moved slowly, loading people onto the ship from big barges with high wire fences on the sides like floating tennis courts. The skippers of some big boats that managed to get alongside jumped aboard with their passengers and let the craft, that must have represented their life's work, drift away. There was a dog on one of them, howling.

At about 3 P.M. the marines had to open fire to scare away a fleet of more than fifty boats, but one man jumped overboard from his small craft and swam for us and made it. An old woman slipped and fell between a boat and the loading barge and a sailor jumped into the crunch between the two vessels to try to save her. But she was squashed into a red pulp and they took the mess out to sea in a tug and dumped it overboard.

Just after four, a South Vietnamese helicopter, with three men aboard and two motorcycles strapped to its seats, began to circle the ship. The men signaled frantically for us to clear the foredeck for a landing, but it was too crowded. We couldn't move more than two feet in the crush of people.

The pilot made about five circuits of the deck and we thought he'd land and kill us but then he decided to put down on one of the barges beside the ship. The crowd on the barge scattered as he made an almost perfect landing. But his rotor hit the top of the high wire fencing around the barge and broke into small pieces like shrapnel which peppered the decks of the *Sgt. Miller*. A few refugees were slightly injured.

Then angry marines pulled the three men, apparently not seriously injured, from the chopper and turned hoses on it. The motor was roaring and sparking as it tried to drive the broken rotor through the wires of the barge. The marines turned their guns on the pilot and forced him back into the cockpit to turn it off. They they pushed the helicopter into the sea. Within ten minutes we were loading refugees again.

By nightfall we had taken on about 4,000 more refugees and the work continued throughout the night. On the foredeck we were given one paper cup of water during the day and at night a small meal of shredded fish and rice.

Our main trouble was that we hadn't planned to be refugees in the first place. The other refugees, or at least most of them, were somewhat prepared with awnings, a few hammocks, groundsheets, water containers, and even toothpaste and soap. Some of them had been on the road down from Hue and Da Nang for more than a month and knew and cherished the necessities of survival. But we had only the bush jacket suits we had been wearing for two days. Sullivan and I struggled for space near the bow of the ship, leaning on the gunwhale and talked of our troubles.

"What do you think our main problem is?" I asked in an attempt to get down to basics.

148

"My main problem is I'm split up from my crew," he replied. "I lost them in the scramble at Tan Son Nhut. They must have got on another chopper and gone to another ship and by now they're probably having tea in the officers' wardroom. But the idiots back at the BBC will never understand."

There is something very pathetic about a TV reporter who has lost his camera crew and for a while I thought Sullivan was going to weep. But he was, in fact, a very tough, able, and practical man and that was the closest he went to losing his cool and his middle-class British stiff upper lip in the hard days and nights of what became a long voyage.

"You could do radio when you get back," I said in an attempt at consolation. "We'll probably both have a good story if we survive this thing."

"Radio, shit," he said. "You've got to do it on TV and you can't do that without a crew. In the meantime let's try to make sure we survive so that the bastards back at the BBC will at least get a chance to abuse me."

I began to like Sullivan and our friendship deepened as the voyage continued and got tougher. For a while we discussed what talents we had that might help us keep alive on an open deck, in the tropical sun, with apparently no food or water, but most of them were similar journalistic talents; abilities to talk to anybody, to remember facts, to make friends and contacts, to judge situations quickly, to keep calm and detached, none of which seemed to help much in the present circumstances. So we began to explore each other's private lives and hobbies.

"For a hobby I make model Tiger Moths," Sullivan said. "Not just any sort of model airplane, only Tiger Moths. I'm a specialist."

"Christ," I said. And we both laughed. But we

agreed that it might help if we had to glue pieces of wood together for a raft, or something, if we had any glue.

In fact, in the long nights that followed, it helped considerably. As a kid at the end of the Second World War I had flown Tiger Moths briefly. So later when we were hungry we almost always got to talking about Tiger Moths, how they flew and what they could do. We argued about their stalling speed and their reaction to various acrobatics. Tiger Moths cemented our friendship and kept us sane.

"My hobby is sailing," I told him. "I know a bit about boats. I've got my own sloop back in Hong Kong. I go sailing to get away from it all. I'm fond of the sea. Or at least, I was."

We both laughed again, but we agreed that we might be able to make use of my small knowledge of navigation if there was a mutiny on the *Sgt. Miller* and that my ability with knots and splices and experiences with winds and weather could come in handy.

As we talked, other "round-eyes" appeared from among the thousands of Vietnamese on the decks and began to gather around us. A totally exhausted Spanish TV crew, who had also been on the *Denver*, came first, clutching a camera for which they had no film.

Then, through the night came:

René Schiller, a nice, crazy, emotional, middle-aged Frenchwoman who lived in London and had gone to Vietnam in the week before it fell to pick up an orphan for adoption. She was holding the hand of a scruffy-looking, six-year-old, half-French, half-Vietnamese boy when she approached us. He spoke only Vietnamese and she called him simply "the kid." So did we. He was a good boy and eventually he learned to call us "uncle."

Anne-Marie Disloquez, a French-Vietnamese girl of about twenty-four with a wonderful smile, no bra, and big breasts almost bursting through the man's shirt she was wearing. She would never tell us about her background or what she did for a living in Saigon, but it was fairly obvious. "I like helping people, making people happy," she used to say when we asked her what she had been doing in Saigon and why she was leaving her homeland.

Mike Van Zyl, a tough South African engineer, who had lost even his passport in the mess of the evacuation and was wearing the same shirt and trousers, now split embarrassingly up the back from crotch to waist, that he was wearing when he started running from the central coast city of Nha Trang two weeks before.

Akira Hayashi, first secretary in the Japanese embassy in Saigon, who was probably the most unwilling refugee on the ship. He had been on normal diplomatic business at the U.S. Embassy in Saigon when it was surrounded by mobs of rioting Vietnamese. The Americans had pushed him protesting into a helicopter and sent him out, still in his neat diplomatic suit and tie. Then they kicked him off the *Denver* because he didn't have a passport and he ended up on the *Sgt. Miller* with the Vietnamese refugees and his diplomatic briefcase. He was calm, but a little confused.

There was also a very loud-mouthed American man who never told us his name but had been in Vietnam buying scrap metal. He had a habit of shouting such things as "Women and children first," and "If you ARVN had fought better we wouldn't be here." Nobody knew why he was really there and he was no help to us at all. After a few days, he vanished from our group to survive alone somewhere near the stern of the ship.

As the dawn rose, Sullivan and I called a meeting of this bedraggled (except for the still elegant Japanese diplomat) group and we proposed that we should form ourselves into a round-eye family. The Vietnamese, we pointed out, were surviving as family units, protecting the positions they had staked out on the deck and sharing whatever they had, including moral and practical support.

Sullivan and I became the grandfather and father. We never could work out who was which, although in the end I seemed to be mostly trying to proclaim grandfatherly philosophies and calming people while Sullivan was thrust into the more practical, fatherly role which he handled with British aplomb. The two women, collectively, made a long-suffering, frequently courageous, often emotional, but nice mother. The Spaniards slept a lot and did little of a practical nature. Van Zyl seemed to fit easily into the role of eldest son, sometimes unruly and critical, but often of great assistance. The diplomat turned out to be like a visiting uncle, who felt somewhat out of place among such a strange family, and detached from it, although he was willing to give occasional advice.

Our first decision as a "family" was to claim a position whch we would defend as our "home," and we chose one on the foredeck, mainly because it was the only space available. It was a coiled piece of thick Manila rope—the forward mooring line—which stretched beside the gunwale for about ten feet and into the deck for about five feet. It was unlevel and uncomfortable, and as the sailor expert of the family I advised that we'd be the first washed off the deck if a storm blew up, but it was the best we could do.

The sea was now glassy calm. Flying fish skimmed the smooth surface. Water snakes slid eerily beneath it. The sun hit down from above and reflected up again from the steel deck so that it would have been impossible to survive for more than a few hours without cover. We were thirsty.

The ship was still picking up refugees from the hundreds of sampans surrounding it, but now we had caught up with the main American fleet of about thirty ships, half of them battleships, half refugee carriers and supply ships. We were the last U.S. ship out of Vietnamese waters.

As a "family" we decided that our most immediate need was for some form of cover, not only to protect us from the dehydrating sun, but so we could establish an area that would be our home and which we would defend against the crush that was growing continually worse. It was more important for us to have cover than anyone else. Our skins were fair and we were not accustomed, as many of the Vietnamese were, to long days in the open fields. The bald spot at the back of my head was already burnt by the morning sun and there was not even a handkerchief among us big enough to cover it.

We felt different and probably superior to the other refugees at this time and deserving of some special treatment. So the group decided that Sullivan and I should use our journalistic talents to talk our way into the officers' quarters and ask for blankets and sheets and string to make an awning. But when we got near to the crews' quarters two big marines stationed on the bridge pointed automatic rifles at us and yelled nervously, "Get back, get back." So we got back.

Anne-Marie suggested she might have some talents more useful than ours. She combed her long black hair, brushed as much mud as possible off her tight blue jeans and undid the top button of her shirt. "Viens," she told René Schiller in her Vietnamese French. And the two women struggled and pushed their way through the human mass toward the bridge.

Within an hour they were back. They had six sheets and a ball of string, pillow cases to make covers for our heads and a plastic bag of water.

René had a plate of chicken legs stolen from the officers' mess, where she had very briefly talked herself into a job in the galley.

Anne-Marie produced, like a magician, a small bottle of brandy, a pack of cigars, and a can of deodorant spray. She smiled and said nothing when we asked how she got them.

Much later I was presented with a National Newspaper Award for a story I wrote about this voyage and the citation stressed my "professionalism." But it was Anne-Marie's professionalism that saved our lives.

It was ridiculous. We spent ten minutes spraying ourselves and our filthy clothes with the deodorant. Despite fatherly warnings from Sullivan and me that it might be needed in an emergency, the Spaniards insisted on drinking the brandy, so we shared it. And we smoked the cigars.

Somebody joked about going for a stroll around the deck. Somebody of course suggested we should ask the chief steward if we could change our table.

We took turns to sleep on the coil of rope, three at a time. And in the morning we built our tent from the sheets and the string.

But it was not a good day. Despite the small tent where we could get some relief for a while, the sun seemed to be worse and there was no water until noon when a marine gave us two cups each from a plastic gasoline container. The marines also built six little platforms out of four-by-fours which they hung over the side of the ship for use as toilets, but there was a constant line-up, at least twenty yards long, for each of them and they were an esthetic and gymnastic challenge.

For toilet paper we used thousand piastre bills which were not very efficient but at least gave me an excuse later for one of my more exotic expense accounts: "For wiping arse on thousand piastre bills . . ."

The worst thing that day was that both women began to have their periods and there were no sanitary napkins on board. A doctor who moved occasionally among the refugees gave them each a small piece of cotton wool but it was not enough and in the end Sullivan and I had to tear up our only sweaty singlets for them.

The ship was a stink, a crush, a rattling noise. Down the holds it was worse. The holds smelled of urine and sweat. Families were crowded so tight in them they could hardly move. It was so hot down there you could see the air. Hot, stinking air is yellow or purple. The people lay on sheets of plastic on the steel deck. Babies were crying constantly. They were given a cup of milk in the mornings and some hot water later in the day.

We were better off on deck and our little house made of sheets stood up despite a bit of a breeze made by the ship's movement.

We were all thirsty, but for some reason we couldn't manage to eat all of the meal of rice mixed with sardines the marines dished out from garbage cans that night.

The sea remained glassy smooth and the sun seemed to hover only a few hundred feet over the little ship, concentrating all its rays in an attempt to broil alive the dirty, crowded cargo of pathetic people.

We were four days out from Saigon now, heading, we believed for Guam, about ten days away, and it seemed obvious many wouldn't make it that far.

The Vietnamese lay on the hot decks or in the even hotter holds. They were quiet now and you could hear the creaking of the ship. Even the babies were silent. There seemed to be no cries left in them any more as they curled around their exhausted mothers.

Eerily there was no breeze on the deck where we

were. I had told our round eye family that part of the risk of our position on the foredeck would be offset because we would catch a cooling breeze caused by the ship's movement through the still air. But this must have been neutralized by a following wind equal to the five or six knots the ship was traveling. So we were in this strange and dangerous stillness. There was only the heat.

Sometimes the silence was shattered briefly. ARVN soldiers in their tattered uniforms fought among themselves for a scrap of food they had saved, their last cigarette, or a little more space on the deck. They had no weapons and not much energy. Either the marines moved among the brawling soldiers wielding rifle butts or older, wiser civilian refugees intervened.

In mid afternoon, Anne-Marie, who had seemed the most cheerful of our "family," climbed slowly and in complete silence from a bollard to the top of the gunwale and she seemed to have actually left the ship in a suicide attempt when the Spanish cameraman leaped from the coil of rope, grabbed her ankles and hurled her harshly back to the deck, scattering a group of slumbering refugee children and bruising her hip and thigh badly.

Anne-Marie was sobbing. "I had twenty-four beautiful dresses. I worked hard for my dresses. I had to leave them behind."

"The cameraman kissed her. We told her there would be more dresses in France or Canada, or wherever. The Vietnamese families around us pretended to ignore the embarrassment of disruption in ours. Eventually Anne-Marie smiled through her tears and the silence enveloped us again.

There was nothing to do but lie, when it was your turn, on the coil of rope, or stand in the hot stillness staring at the slimy water snakes below or the skimming flying fish.

Some were worse off than we were. By now many

of the children had diarrhea and an infectious disease called pink eye, which fills the eyes with ugly pus. They whimpered quietly. Others were badly dehydrated. They lay still near their mothers. None of them died. Four babies were born, but none near our place on the foredeck.

Two French women, a mother and daughter, the owners of the Guillaume Tell Restaurant in Saigon where we correspondents ate often, had at first inveigled their way into the crew's quarters, but now under the policy of complete equality for all refugees of all races they had been expelled to the deck and were worse off than most because they had missed their chance to find a space and build a tent. They huddled together all day in a tiny space against a bulkhead, heads bowed under big, formerly fashionable hats.

Near us an Irish nun and a Vietnamese nun with a British passport sat stoically out in the sun under their black veils in their hot black habits, sometimes counting their beads, occasionally moving among the Vietnamese families, offering help with the children. The Irish nun was a big woman and we had no room for her on the coil of rope. We were being invaded at nights anyway as the other refugee families tried to spread out just a foot or two and crushed us against the gunwale. Twice Renée Schiller woke up at night with a Vietnamese man sleeping on top of her. "I assumed I was going to be raped," said Renée, "but I wasn't. The poor guys just wanted something soft to sleep on. Danmed insulting. They moved away politely when I pointed out they were crushing me."

Despite this we asked the nuns if they would like to sit occasionally under out tent and maybe sleep there for a while, but they refused. They could not go to the toilet boards hanging over the side of the ship, the Irish nun explained. Their habits were too awkward for the climb overboard and anyway she personally was not agile enough. In the circumstances they had had several "accidents" and they did not want to embarrass us.

We didn't see much of the marines except when they came to our part of the ship to bring our occasional ration of a plastic cup of water and the one meal of the day, rice mixed with a little meat or fish, distributed from plastic garbage cans. They were tough men with bulging biceps but many of them were amazingly kind and gentle with the children and some were pleasant to us and apparently concerned about us. They brought us salt pills and occasionally sneaked us extra little plastic bags of water.

"It's the slave ship syndrome, man," one Black marine corporal told us. "Us Americans have never got over the slave ship days." Then he laughed hilariously and offered a lifesaving handout of salt pills.

Some of the marines were not so nice.

"You guys had better remember that you're all just refugees to us," one young crew-cut character lectured us for no apparent reason. "Everybody's the same on this ship. All refugees. All the same. No special privileges," he warned.

Sometimes, for some reason, the food didn't come, at least to our end of the ship, for periods exceeding twenty-six hours and there were rumblings of revolt among some of the hungry refugees and plans made to assault the galley, but always the handout of rice mixed with bully beef or whatever arrived just in time and often, oddly, sometimes we round eyes couldn't eat all of our small ration. The hunger was not too bad but the thirst was. My hand would shake like an alcoholic's as I lifted the plastic cup to dry lips. It was warm, sometimes hot, but it was very, very good.

Now the ship smelled like a wet diaper. More kids had pus in their eyes and they were wimpering. But a rumor swept through the deck that we would be going to Subic Bay, the big U.S. naval base in the Philippines, instead of Guam, another four or five days away. The sun on the deck and the filth in the holds would have killed many in those extra days and we round eyes, selfishly perhaps, asked a marine to take a note to the captain, telling him who we were and our nationalities, and asking that if, in fact, we were calling at Subic Bay, we be allowed to get off. There was no reply.

Another day and then a landfall. We though it must be the Philippines. Vietnamese asked us, but we didn't know.

"Maybe it is," I told at least a score of them who for some reason seemed to think we should know. "Maybe they'll let us all off," I said. "Maybe they'll just let the sick off and take the rest of us on to Guam. I don't know.

A woman near us, who had quietly cared for her family of four children, a grandmother and grandfather, but no husband, throughout the voyage, suddenly began to weep. "We won't make it to Guam," she said quietly in good French. "The children won't make it to Guam. How far is it to Guam?" She wasn't sobbing or wailing, just weeping, and she covered her eyes so the children and the old people wouldn't see.

Others pushed through the crush and lined the gunwales staring at the land in silence.

The ship pulled in alongside a dock in the Subic Bay naval base. But we still didn't know whether we would be allowed off or would be going on to Guam. Sullivan and I thought it was likely we would just take on food and water, then move on. After all, we had been kicked off the *Denver* because we couldn't go to the Philippines. But we didn't say anything to the others. And then marines began carrying the sick from the ship on stretchers and our black friend who laughed about slave ships told us that third-country nationals would be allowed ashore next.

There were cold Cokes on the dock. I don't like Coke. It was beautiful. An air force captain saw us and shouted to some sailors, "Hey, some VIPs here. Look after them." It felt better than being a refugee.

The air force captain told us the Vietnamese would also be allowed off the ship eventually, that seebees (civilians) had been working frantically for a week erecting tents for them and that they would be "processed" and fed and rested and then later, probably, they'd go on to Guam. Nice, fresh, clean American ladies, the wives of officers and sailors, kept pushing food and cigarettes on us. A security officer, Captain Bill Darrow, produced a guitar and played flamenco for the Spanish TV crew. Then he sang "Saigon Girls" and a soft love song to Anne-Marie, who hadn't lost her talents. She subtly undid the top button of her shirt and turned her brown Vietnamese eyes on him.

It was hard to remember then that there were no Saigon girls any more and Saigon was Ho Chi Minh City; that the Hondas would be silent and Tu Do Street empty of almost everything but political idealism. Anne-Marie seemed sadly symbolic. Saigon had seduced the French and almost ruined the Americans. It is a whore of a city that will one day corrupt even the Communists. And it seemed a long way away then as the marine sang his love song to the dark-haired girl and she smiled that sly Saigon smile.

Darrow escorted our smelly, bedraggled little group in a ferry to the main part of the base where officers and their wives checked our identities with great and kindly American efficiency, gave us soap, toothpaste, and towels for a shower in a gymnasium, and told us it was likely we would be able to go to

Manila next day. A young officer and his wife took the two women to their home for the night and informed the rest of us, with many apologies, we would have to sleep just one more night on a ship. The officer drove us in a jeep to the *Denver*, moored at a dock.

The same cheerful young lieutenant who had checked us in from the Saigon choppers and then had to kick us off the ship, met us at the top of the gangway. "Jesus," he said. "I'm glad you're OK. Christ Almighty. Hey, welcome aboard. It's great to see you. I'll get you a good cabin. I'll tell the captain you're here."

I have never been angry, not even then, about the original events on the *Denver*. It was just stupidity. After all the Americans got us out of Saigon one way or another. They got me out of Da Nang. They would in the long run have got me out of Phnom Penh. They didn't really have to do anything at all.

But Mike Van Zyl, the tough South African with the split pants was angry. "You can tell the captain," he told the cheerful lieutenant, "to stick his battleship right up his arse."

CHAPTER 10

# The Great and Beloved Leader

We do some things wrong in the Western press but we are not even in the same league as the North Koreans when it comes to slanting a story.

One of the first leads (a lead is journalists' jargon for the opening line, paragraph, or incident of a story) I saw on a story from North Korea read: "America's dirty president, Richard Nixon, uttered another incredible piffle today." I thought it was quaint with a somewhat more obvious bias than any Western editor would accept. The story had something to do with Watergate.

To cover South Asia it was necessary to read the (North) Korean Central News Agency (KCNA) releases, along with the wires from many other government-run agencies, in the hope that a little bit of truth would emerge sometimes from between the lines and sometimes, indeed, it did.

Haptong, the South Korean News Agency, could be counted on, of course, to say exactly the opposite of KCNA, but its reporters obviously accepted that the reader had some intelligence, and they therefore occasionally included a fact. The New China News Agency (NCNA) provided insights into occurrences and changes in the vast mainland through an amazing outpouring of verbatim speeches and passages from the official papers and magazines, while the Central News Agency of Taiwan (CNA) produced, ever so seldom, a real little pearl of probable truth in its ocean of propaganda. Kyodo, the Japanese news agency, was westernized, efficient and generally factual. But on a busy day it was best just to ignore KPL, the Pathet Lao News Agency, Antara, the Indonesian News Agency, Montsame, the Mongolian News Agency, and others like them. They only added to the confusion or created more of it.

There was never any confusion about the stuff that poured from the North Korean agency though. It was straight, unadulterated, amazingly blatant, interesting, unbelievable often hilarious propaganda, almost all of it concentrated on the canonization in his lifetime of the Great and Beloved Leader, Kim Il Sung.

Day after day, story after story, Kim used the wire service to exhalt himself as his country's "peerless patriot, national hero, ever-victorious, iron-willed, brilliant commander, great thinker, theoretician, strategist and philosopher."

"His knowledge is matchless," proclaimed one clipping I kept for the fun of it. "He even has a deep knowledge of medicine . . . with occult powers, not only seeing through earth and water, but also the minds of others, and able to fly over the sky at will by utilizing a method to contract space."

Kim, one of the veteran leaders in the Communist bloc (only Albania's Enver Hoxa and Yugoslavia's Joseph Tito have lasted longer in power) was described in my Korea-watching days as a playwright, a songwriter, and expert in all affairs from office management to egg-laying. More recently he seems, according to his wire service, to have acquired the ability to bring the dead back to life.

Any words he utters are printed in the Pyongyang papers in red ink and when there seemed to be a move to set up his son, Kim Jung Il, as the heir apparent, Kim Junior's words appeared in special blue ink. Kim once rode the Pyongyang subway; the seat is now draped in satin and the car travels the rails empty as a memorial to his presence.

As a result of this sort of thing, Kim has, of course, begun to believe it himself, as people with managerial or political power in the West often come to believe in their exaggerated images. This makes him dangerous.

Because of this constant barrage of baloney, the whole party, the whole country and its fifteen million people, are firmly united like a single-celled biological organism, breathing, thinking, and acting only in accordance with the revolutionary ideas of the great leader. It is an example of propaganda-created ideological unity without precedent in any other society in the East or West, in any age. It makes the efforts of Hitler and Goebbels in Nazi Germany seem amateurish in comparison.

Inside North Korea, as a result of the brainwashing, Kim receives a frenzied welcome whenever he appears. Men punch the air and women collapse in hysteria. A huge, sixty-five foot high bronze statue of the Great and Beloved Leader dominates the skyline of Pyongyang and there is another one north of Panmunjom, the neutral ground between the two Koreas, so huge it is visible through binoculars from miles away. He has turned himself into a political icon. And he has turned his people into a nation of mindless puppets.

Most of the robots produced by this control of information seldom emerge from their closeted country, but a few do about once a month at the military armistice meetings that have been droning endlessly on at Panmunjom since the 1953 ceasefire in the Korean War.

Panmunjom is in the demilitarized zone between North and South Korea. The armistice meetings are held in a little hut, across a table divided by a microphone wire that lies exactly along the center of the DMZ near the 38th parallel. Strange and silly things happen in this hut and around it.

In the beginning the United Nations flag at the conference table was a little higher than the North Korean flag so the Communists brought a bigger flag. This caused an escalation in flagstick sizes until eventually an agreement was reached, after much debate, to standardize them. Then the North Koreans put a thicker pad of felt under their standard-size flagstick.

At one stage the North Koreans were alleged to have sawed several inches from the legs of the Americans' wooden chairs to bring their taller opponents down to size at the conference table. Some historians say this story is apocryphal, but in any event both sides now use metal chairs.

For many years the meetings at Panmunjom went on for hours without a break so that the side with the weaker bladders began to lose more of their concentration. Both sides brought bottles to the meetings and strapped plastic tubes inside their trousers. Then an agreement was reached, after another long debate, providing for a twenty-minute rest period every three hours.

A few years ago the Koreans painted the roofs of their buildings in the joint security compound a special color on which they had trained pigeons to land. "Look," they told the Americans, "even the doves of peace won't land on your buildings." It took the

Americans months to work out what was happening. Then they painted their roofs the same color and the birds landed everywhere.

The meetings inside the little hut are mad. I was covering them in June, 1975. One day, a North Korean spokesman, a sour faced major-general the Americans called Smiley, was reading, over and over again, statements prepared in Pyongyang accusing "you U.S. imperialist agressors and the South Korean puppet clique" of "brutal atrocities." The UN side, led by Major-General William Webb of the U.S. Army, was continually asking what the alleged atrocities were and urging joint investigation of them. But he got nowhere.

The real drama at this 363rd session of the armistice meetings, was outside the little hut, the only place in the world where North Koreans and Americans mix. The tough, diminutive Korean Army guards had knuckles calloused to a thickness of about half an inch from punching trees in toughening-up exercises, so that their fists were deadly knuckledusters of human tissue. They were playing a frightening game.

Whenever one of the American guards, all specially chosen for their height of well over six feet and their tested abilities to keep calm under provocation, became isolated from his comrades for some reason, three or four of the little Koreans would shuffle, ever so slowly, toward him, snarling, spitting, and attempting to create an incident. The Americans maintained the calm demanded of them by their officers. Occasionally a big boot lashed out suddenly to connect with a Korean shin or stomp on a foot. But the Koreans ignored this and continued the intimidating shuffle until they were almost pressing against the lonely guard, their faces leering in contemptuous victory when the American moved away.

These little men, wearing their Kim Il Sung badges on baggy uniforms, are among the uglier examples of what happens when the human mind is first isolated from fact and then persistently fed on false information.

In Kim Il Sung's Korea, the control of the minds of men extends, of course, to attitudes to Western countries. The word American, for instance, seldom appears in the North Korean press. Instead the United States is called *Mije*, a compound of the first syllables of the Korean words for America and imperialism. People use it in about the same way American southerners said Damn Yankee in the post Civil War period.

A favorite sketch performed at the Children's Palace in Pyongyang is titled: *Let's tear the limbs off the U.S. Imperialists*. It features a team of juvenile sharpshooters blasting to bits the cut-out figure of an American military policeman. As a result of this sort of thing, anti-American feeling probably runs deeper in North Korea than in any place in the world.

And it shows in the snarling faces of these puppets of Panmunjom.

There were about twenty alleged North Korean journalists covering this meeting and the brainwashing showed in their faces as well. Ian Ward, of the London *Daily Telegraph*, and I were the only Western journalists there, along with some South Koreans. When we approached the windows of the armistice hut the North Korean journalists surreptitiously stabbed us with their pens and pushed us aside. I am used to the seemingly undignified scrums of the Western media covering a major event. They can be rough but there is humor and goodwill in most of them. The writer ducks for the still photographer and the still photographer ducks for the TV man. There is order and professionalism despite the intense competition. But here there was just a frightening hate.

It annoyed me. The whole situation at Panmunjom annoyed me. As reporters in Cambodia and Vietnam we had been fighting a war of our own, not with the guns and napalm of the soldiers but a war for the truth, against odds created by deceptive, overambitious, bureaucracies, lying military machines, and, in the end, enormous amounts of apathy at home, after the men who run the TV networks in New York made their executive decision that the war was over and switched it off.

It might sound simplistically corny, but it is a fact that the reporters who covered the Indochina wars believed in the truth. They were the top professionals and it is impossible to become a successful reporter without this belief. Some of us failed sometimes, some more often than others. But nobody survives on the respectable papers for long if his facts are wrong, and most covering this era had been reporters a long time. It is not simply a moral question: in a world full of deception the truth can be a gimmick and its telling is often sensational.

The other war the journalists fought was for the free flow of information in the world; the right to pronounce a series of facts, favorable or unfavorable to the people in power, so that the intelligent men, with access to other information, could interpret them and make up their own minds about their meaning and significance.

It is sometimes hard to explain, even to the comfortable, insulated journalistic generals at home, the importance of this war and the rarity of real knowledge in a world where control of information is the source of real power and where even the United Nations Educational, Scientific, and Cultural Organization (UNESCO) is moving ominously toward approval of a motion proclaiming that the work of journalists is the responsibility of governments.

But in the journalistic trenches we understood,

and we cared. The generals safe at home in the editorial offices have never seen what the brainwashing of a despot like Kim Il Sung can do to the beautiful mind of man.

These thoughts were in the back of my mind this day at Panmunjom and they made me do a stupid thing.

When the North Korean journalists stabbed at me with their pens and shoved I shoved them back and I swore at them. I seldom swear. This day I stood where I was and faced the little men in baggy western suits who should have been my colleagues. "Fuck off," I said. And they understood.

Then, later, as I walked from the hut to get a drink of water, I was isolated in the center of the square. Four North Korean soldiers surrounded me, standing about twenty feet away. The other "Western" journalists, Ian Ward and the South Koreans, vanished from the square and I heard Ward shout from a balcony of the U.N. headquarters: "Move, Jack, move, you stupid bastard." I was damned if I was going to move.

The Korean soldiers began their slow shuffle, occasionally cracking their calloused knuckles, big metal badges with pictures of the Great and Beloved Leader shining on their tunics, sometimes spitting on the ground in contempt and uttering one short sound, more a grunt than a word.

It took maybe half an hour. They moved not much more than an inch at a time and their movements were hardly perceptible. The face of the front one, who was the smallest, was contorted into a snarl. He stared unblinkingly at my face, then down at the camera hanging at my chest, and up to my face again.

The ridiculous exercise brought a grim tension to the compound. Other North Korean soldiers watched in silent, staring, groups. In the background, the tall U.S. soldiers were standing stiffly at attention, but occasionally they flashed an encouraging grin that contrasted enormously with the almost inhuman hate and anger in the eyes of the Koreans.

The truce talks droned on inside the little hut, but the Western participants told me later that all of their attention was riveted, through the big windows, on the crazy drama outside.

When the nearest face was about two feet away I lifted the Nikon slowly and tried to focus it. The face was so close to the wide-angle lens it was distorted. I took a picture anyway. The face filled even more of the lens. I took another picture and the face stayed where it was.

"Thanks," I said as calmly as possible. "Thanks very much." And then I used the only Korean phrase I know, *con sum haneda*, which means thank you.

The man made the grunting noise again and spat at my feet.

I pulled a pack of cigarettes from my bush jacket and offered him one. Then quickly, not this man, but one of his colleagues jumped forward and grabbed my jacket and tugged me toward him. The anger in his expression was almost unbelievable. He raised a fist with gnarled knuckles.

"Sir," a huge U.S. Army officer, Major Bill Henderson, was suddenly saying. "Sir, we would like you to continue to keep calm. Or if you are not calm, please continue to appear so." The major was so big he blocked everything else from view.

"I'm calm," I said. "They're not calm."

"Sir," Henderson said, "what occurred was a physical contact and is therefore what we call an incident. Now, sir, we do not want these incidents to develop. I suggest, sir," he continued, "that you do not offer any more cigarettes. In the meantime I am going to stand here next to you for just as long as you want to continue to stand where you are." He was grinning.

The little men moved away backward, their heads down, their face lost. The big American guards, forced by training to move away from the Koreans, were all grinning.

A Turkish colonel walked from the hut and placed a hand on my shoulder. "We were all watching," he said. "We couldn't do anything else but watch. It was like, what's that film, *High Noon*? I wanted to express my admiration."

It was my day for swearing. "Fuck them, colonel," I said.

"Yes," he said. "Fuck the little bastards." He patted my shoulder and walked away.

"You stupid bastard," Ian Ward said. "You nice, stupid, bastard."

The Canadian representative at the talks asked me to join the Western observers for a drink at the officers' mess. It was the 166, 515th "incident" at Panmunjom.

It was the silliest thing I did as a foreign correspondent and the closest I came, despite bombs and bullets, to serious injury. It is the job of the correspondent to get his story, but to remain uninvolved, where possible, physically and emotionally, and especially to keep away from unnecessary trouble. I should have moved away.

Two weeks later I heard the bulletin bells ring on the machine that brought the Reuters wire service into our home in Hong Kong and ripped off the story: "More than a dozen North Korean guards and newsmen attacked two American military men at the truce village of Panmunjom today as the Military Armistice Commission was meeting.

"The incident stemmed from an argument between a U.S. Army major and a North Korean newsman which developed into a fist fight. The officer and a U.S. military policeman who rushed to his aid were seriously injured. Eventually about 230 U.S. soldiers and 120 North Koreans were involved in the melee.

"The officer, Major William Henderson, and the military policeman were knocked unconscious and carried away on stretchers. Major Henderson was punched in the throat and suffered a severe injury to his larynx. There is doubt if he will ever be able to speak again."

I could still see those deadly knuckles, calloused from punching trees.

Marie came into the home-office as she often did when she heard the wire machine bells ring their urgency, and told me I looked pale.

She took the paper from my hand and read it.

"That's the major who saved you," she said.

I was in Sri Lanka covering the conference of about seventy nonaligned nations in June the next year when two U.S. officers were chopped to death by thirty North Korean guards, wielding axes and metal spikes, as the Americans were supervising the trimming of trees in the buffer zone. The *Star*'s managing editor phoned me in Colombo to ask if I thought the incident would start the Third World War. I remembered the patience of the Americans at Panmunjom and I told him I thought not. But I could have been wrong. The Korean peninsula, despite some American troop withdrawals, remains the most potentially explosive area in Asia. It is well known by all correspondents briefed on U.S. strategy, that the Americans, although they deny it officially, are ready to react with strategic nuclear arms when the attack comes.

The 1976 Sri Lanka conference also was the occasion for the first emergence abroad in many years of a large group of North Koreans. There was speculation

172

for a while that The Great and Beloved Leader himself would be coming, but he didn't. He sent instead about fifty diplomatic and military robots in a white ship on which they lived, separated even from colleagues at the conference, and stepping onshore only occasionally.

Ian Ward was there too, along with most other Western correspondents in the area, greeting me as he always has since the Panmunjom incident with a sad head shake and, "Hello, you stupid bastard!"

One day in mid-conference he came to me at the press center, looking strangely serious for him, and asking for my help. "Those little buggers are going to kill someone," he said. "If they don't do it physically they'll frighten him to death."

He led me to a table where the sole South Korean newsman at the conference was sitting. He was probably a KCIA (Korean Central Intelligence Agency) man, but what the hell. The Canadian first secretary at the New Delhi embassy was also accredited to the conference as a correspondent. So was half the CIA.

The South Korean was shaking with fear. Four North Koreans in dark business suits had surrounded him and begun their frightening shuffle. Koreans don't sweat. This one was sweating.

"Friend," Ward said to the South Korean, "would you like to get out of here? If you do we will help you."

The man's knees were wobbly when he stood up. He didn't say a word. Ward and I took an elbow each and led him through the cordon of North Koreans and out through a rear entrance of the press center to a taxi. He never came back to the conference again.

# CHAPTER 11

# You're a better 'ack than I am, Gunga Din!

Prime Minister Indira Gandhi's main problem, apart from her own acute megalomania, was that her people simply wouldn't shut up.

Like many people afflicted by power, in politics and business, she surrounded herself with sycophants and thus separated herself from the realities of her vast and diverse land, India.

When she declared her death-to-democracy, draconian, State of Emergency in June, 1975, she even thought, in her ivory tower, that she could silence the constant murmur of voices that sing-songs across the country and characterizes it, babbling away in the rich hotel lobbies, the coffee shops of the intellectuals, the poor, little villages, even in the shanties of Calcutta where the people still talk as they starve.

This was her worst misjudgement. She threw 20,000 people in jail in an attempt to stifle all opposition, censored the press so that it could say nothing but good about herself, her policies, and her corrupt son

Sanjay, but she failed dismally to make the Indian people, and especially the Indian journalists, stop talking.

Many of the Indian journalists were jailed and some tortured under the dictatorial emergency laws. A few followed the official line laid down by the information minister, V. C. Shukla. But most adapted themselves to the situation as professionally as they could by writing what they were told to write in newspapers nobody believed any more, then talking their heads off, spilling the real beans, to the foreign correspondents. Often they did this bravely in hotel rooms or newspaper offices they firmly believed to be bugged, as if they were ashamed of not being jailed along with their other honest colleagues. In this way, between us, we were able to get the facts out to the free world one way or another.

I found the best way to beat the censorship early in the emergency was simply to telephone Toronto from my hotel room which was supposed, everybody said, to be bugged. The overseas operator invariably and politely apologized for a delay of up to ten hours on the calls.

"Madam," I would say in tones of great authority, "this is an urgent, top-priority, uncensored press call."

She would then put the call through immediately. Often there were other correspondents in the room when I made my "urgent uncensored" calls and they would break into such a loud state of hilarity, the bug, if it was there, would have been useless.

Martin Woollacott, of *The Guardian*, did much the same thing except that he submitted his copy first to the censors. *The Guardian* would then print the three or four distorted sentences allowed by the censors adjacent to the columns of factual prose he filed on the phone.

One of my best contacts among the talkative Indian journalists was Balran Tandon, a diminutive, brilliant editorial writer and political expert who seemed to be even more ashamed than most because he wasn't in jail with his colleagues.

When I visited Balran in his little office in the newspaper building in New Delhi he would call in his editor, a young man of no apparent editorial ability, who was appointed to his job during the emergency because of his Gandhi connections.

Then while the young editor hung his head in embarrassment or frustration, Balran would produce his notebooks and relate intimate and always accurate details of the Gandhi regime and the political situation which he couldn't get printed in his own paper.

During one of these conversations I mentioned casually that I was searching, as all other correspondents were, for J. P. Narayan, the saintly leader of the underground opposition to the emergency, who had been released from jail and was then in hiding.

This was no trouble for Balran. He produced one of his little black books, gave me the telephone number of Narayan's brother in Bombay and instructed me to phone him. I flew to Bombay, made the call, and was talking to Narayan within a few hours in a dingy little apartment near the Bombay waterfront. The frail old man, beloved by all Indians except for the Gandhi clique, gave me what he called his "last will and testament" so it could be published to the world. It was a long, moving document, bitterly and cleverly condemning Mrs. Gandhi with kind, often almost gentle phrases, and it made the front pages of most of the free world's newspapers.

Mrs. Gandhi kicked at least a dozen correspondents unceremoniously out of the country during this exercise, but I survived for a long while mainly because I pigeoned most of my own copy out to Sri Lanka for filing and it took some time for the results to get back to the censors in Delhi.

The cooperation between Indian journalists like Balran and the foreign correspondents played a major role in ending the Emergency and stifling Mrs. Gandhi's megalomania, at least temporarily. It was celebrated by the correspondents at Delhi's dingy little press club in a piece of doggerel, after Kipling. (A *bhisti* is a factotem; *mushti* is reliable information; *washti wallahs* are secret police.)

Now in Injia's sunny clime,
Where I used to spend me time,
Reportin' on the mess wot she was in,
Of all them blackfaced crew,
The finest man I knew,
Was our editorial *bhisti*, Gunga Din.

While Our Men In Delhi lay,
In the Press Club bar all day,
Complainin' o' the risin' price o' gin,
'E would leave them sweatin' 'acks,
An' go rootin' round for facts,
So they'd 'ave a bit o' *mushti* to put in.

I shan't fergit the night,
When, so sloshed I couldn't write,
The London office came through on the line:
"She 'as bunged 'em all in clink!"
Screamed the Editor, "I think,
You should do eight thousand words by 'alf past
    nine!"

Could I even find the loo,
Let alone remember who,
Was which and which was what and what was
    why?

I sat weepin' in me beer,
Then a soft voice in me ear,
Said, "There really is no need, my friend to
     cry."
          It was Din! Din! Din!
          With his Olivetti ready, Gunga Din!
          And 'is fingers flashed with ease,
          All across them ruddy keys!
          It was *From Our Man in Delhi* (i.e. Din).

Well they chucked me out for that!
" 'Ere's your passport and your 'at,
Now bugger orf on board tomorrer's plane!
And we'll 'ave your 'uman rights
If we catch you in our sights,
Comin' sniffin' round the premises again!"

That was that; but Gunga Din,
'Ad the *washti wallahs* in,
An' they threw 'im in a corrugated van.
So we watched 'im out o' sight,
As 'e vanished in the night,
An' we raised a glass to that 'eroic man!
          Yes, Din! Din! Din!
          You dusky 'eathen scribbler, Gunga Din!
          Though I've belted you an' flayed you,
          By the livin' Gawd that made you,
          You're a better 'ack than I am, Gunga Din!
     One of my other key contacts was also a jour-
nalist, although he was a very ordinary one, without
the class, reputation and contacts of Balran, and he
seemed to be perpetually out of work except for a few
minor "stringer" assignments for a few Indian papers.
As a foreign correspondent I would never have met
Hari Singh except for the fact that I informed the
Canadian High Commission on my first visit to India,

long before the Emergency, that I would like to live with an ordinary Indian family, preferably out in a poor village, so I could get the feel of the real India and try to understand the difficulties and problems of family life.

The idea at first appalled the diplomats in their plush offices on Delhi's embassy row and then intrigued them. Most of them had never met an ordinary Indian themselves. But on instructions from the diplomats a local employee in the press office was able to introduce me to Hari and from then on whenever I covered India I went to live with him, his wife, and two lovely teenage daughters for a few days.

It was not exactly what I had wanted in the first place. They rented a reasonable little house in downtown Delhi and were high-class Brahmins who managed despite Hari's chronic unemployment to keep an untouchable maid. But they were closer to ordinary Indians than most correspondents got. I ate Mrs. Singh's vegetarian food with my fingers and slept in a little bed in a corridor outside the one small bedroom in which they all slept on two mattresses, occasionally joined by a cousin or two. They had a toilet but no toilet paper. We dipped a red plastic mug into the toilet bowl, using the left hand we didn't eat with, and sloshed the water on our bottoms. The water was always cold.

Living together like this we became friends. Mrs. Singh, who didn't speak a word of English treated me like a long-lost son. The two girls, students at a local convent, came to call me "uncle" and Hari was not only proud of his foreign correspondent friend but always considerably relieved when I escorted his wife on her shopping expeditions to the rice store and local "supermarket" and paid the bill from my expense account.

It was quite obvious that Mrs. Singh stocked up the family larder with about a month's supply of ghee and other goodies when we made these shopping trips, but they were well worthwhile journalistically. When Mrs. Gandhi was proclaiming through the censored press during the Emergency that the price of rice and other necessities was dropping because of her courageous leadership, Mrs. Singh was muttering in the stores, showing me the higher bills.

"I wish," she said once through one of the daughters, "somebody would kill that woman."

Mrs. Singh was a gentle, religious soul. I trusted her more than I trusted Mrs. Gandhi. I knew how the Emergency was really progressing, and I wrote it.

Everybody knew I was going to be kicked out of India when I was sent back in June of 1976 to cover the first anniversary of the Emergency. I knew it. All the correspondents in Hong Kong knew it. The Canadian High Commissioner in New Delhi knew. But the office in Toronto seemed to want me to go in order to place a martyr's imprimateur on the tough anti-Gandhi copy I'd filed on two long, previous visits. I had even predicted, correctly as it turned out, that Mrs. Gandhi would be defeated if she ever again dared to call an election. I'd called her son a crook and I'd unleashed J. P. Narayan's "last will and testament" onto the free world. In Canada the Indian government sponsored ethnic newspapers were running page one headlines stating "Toronto Star New Delhi Staffer Should Be Expelled Or Detained." It didn't make any sense at all to me to go back, but the paper insisted, so I went.

I memorized my contact books and destroyed them on the flight from Hong Kong and actually passed through the immigration desk at New Delhi airport with no trouble. But when I was waiting, a little nervously, for my baggage a Sikh immigration official patted my shoulder and asked if I was John Denis

Cahill and if my father was John Lawrence Cahill. It seemed a strange fact to unearth as my father had been dead for many years.

The immigration officials were very friendly and polite about the whole thing. They kept joining their hands in front of their chests and bowing in the Indian gesture of friendship and respect. They kept telling me their orders came from the very top and that I had to be put on the next plane that took off for anywhere in the world. It happened to be going to Frankfurt.

A Canadian diplomat, Norman Macdonnell, who had come to the airport to keep an eye on the situation, argued about the grave effects all of this was having on Canadian-Indian relations until after the Frankfurt plane left, and then the nice immigration men bundled me onto the next plane which, fortunately, was going to Hong Kong, thus saving me from a trip round the world.

The officials lined up as I walked along the tarmac, bowing and smiling and I clasped my hands in front of my chest in the same gesture of respect for each of them.

"We'll see you soon," one of them said. "After the Emergency, come back. It won't last forever."

Mother India is a large, old, ugly, scabby woman with a kind heart and beautiful mind. You either love her or you hate her. It is easier to love her and it is good that her babbling, confusing sing-song voice, and the brave journalists, are free again.

# CHAPTER 12

# On the road

I had been on the road for a long time by the end of summer, 1976. In spring we had all been back to Canada for home leave and talks with editors. We flew the cheap airlines because the deal is that the *Star* pays economy fares for the family at International Air Transport Association (IATA) rates, and that's all.

Hotel rooms, or other forms of accommodation, for a family of six are expensive anywhere in North America so that home leave becomes economically impossible unless at least some of the cost is recovered by bargaining for cheaper fares. So most expatriates in the Far East, not only newsmen, are forced to first argue for hours with their travel agents to find the cheapest tickets available, and use the savings to help pay for accommodation.

Many of the cheap airlines are fine and you can bargain in Hong Kong for tickets on a Korean Air Line 747 or a China Airline (Taiwanese) 707 or even the superior Singapore and Thai airlines that charge about half the IATA rates. It's the longest flight in the world and sometimes there are delays at airports but in many other ways—including free booze, the more charming and helpful attendants in their native dress, and free orchids for the ladies—the Asian airlines are better than the members of the international price fixing group.

For a few weeks we had rented a cottage on the Lake of Bays, about 150 miles from Toronto, in Ontario's beautiful Muskoka district. We sailed and savored the smell of pines and the cool climate.

The earthquake which devastated Tangshan in China, killing more than 600,000 people, occurred during this little holiday and Mark Harrison, then executive editor of the *Star* and since editor of the Montreal *Gazette*, whose cottage was next to ours, reported as we lazed on his dock one weekend that our absence from the Hong Kong base had caused some small confusion in the *Star*'s newsroom.

An editor had read the first wire story of the quake and shouted: "Where's Cahill?"

"He's in the Muskokas," Harrison said.

Every editor in the room, according to Harrison, raised his head and exclaimed in high-pitched, puzzled chorus: "In the Muskokas?"

We had a good rest and took a long, cheap flight back to the heat and hustle of Hong Kong which was home by now.

Then even before the jet lag was over I had to cover the Conference of Non-Aligned Nations in Sri Lanka and after that I had to pick up Allan Maceachen, Canada's external affairs minister and deputy prime minister, on a trip through Southeast Asia and Australasia.

Colombo, capital of Sri Lanka, was hot and crowded with the delegates of many countries. Martin Woollacott of *The Guardian*, Richard Smith of *Newsweek*, and I were booked into a hotel thirty miles out of town. The conference, in many languages, was hard work. And I had some business to do.

On my first trip to Sri Lanka I had gone into the streets of Colombo, the best city in the world for gem buying, to find a sapphire for Marie. The vendors in the little shops in the back alleys are remarkable bargainers, possibly the best in Asia. Conduct of business with them develops into a yelling match within minutes. Counters on which they have laid out their sparkling wares, after bringing them from a safe in envelopes, have to be pounded hard and often. Stores have to be stomped out of in disgust, sometimes several times, before a yelling vendor chases you along an alley and concludes a deal.

But it can be done profitably. If you are patient, vocal and not too dumb you can pick up a sapphire of reasonable color and cut for about twenty-five dollars. Or you can pick up a piece of glass from a milk of magnesia bottle for the same price. But even if you picked up two pieces of glass for every one real sapphire, you weren't doing badly. I always carried a jeweller's eye glass with me and although I couldn't tell the difference between a sapphire and a piece of glass, it made me look like an expert and I only ever ended up with one piece of glass.

I couldn't afford more than a couple of street sapphires a trip, not only because of inability to stretch an expense account, but also because of the inordinate amount of time it took to make a decent deal. And on this first trip, before venturing into the back alleys, I decided to check at the genuine, authorized, expensive jewelers in the Intercontinental Hotel on what size and color of sapphire was worth what at the official rates.

While I was looking at the beautiful cornflower blue and black and white star sapphires on display, the owner of the store, who must have been a millionaire, approached me. He was a little short and a little stout, about the same build as me. He stood beside me and measured out heights. Then he began to pat me and feel the texture of my suit, which was a bush jacket outfit made by Mr. Minh, the correspondents' tailor of Tu Do Street in Saigon, for about twenty dollars.

"How much do you want for your suit?" he asked. Clothing is in very short supply in Sri Lanka.

"I don't want anything for my suit," I said. "I'm just looking at your sapphires."

"Do you have any more suits like that in your room?" he asked. He was persistent and he continued to pat me.

I began to realize that for the first time ever in Asia I was on the strong side of a bargaining position. The guy really wanted my suit, and he owned all of those sapphires.

"These suits are terribly expensive," I said. "I probably paid $300 for this one. It was made by Mr. Minh in Saigon, you know, the best bush jacket tailor in the world." There can be no conscience about lying to an Asian gem dealer, or any other Asian dealer for that matter. He wouldn't expect otherwise.

"Do you see any sapphires you like?" he asked.

I picked up a beautifully cut cornflower blue stone of about five carats, worth maybe $3,000 in Sri Lanka, possibly double that at home.

"That's not bad," I said. But from his genuinely dismal expression I could see I had taken a bit too much of a bargaining position.

"I'd really like your suit," he said. He was almost crying.

We settled for a huge nineteen-carat garnet and a couple of small star sapphires, with a half a dozen moonstones thrown in, and he came to my room in the hotel and almost stripped me of the suit, then began rummaging rudely through the cupboards and baggage for more suits while I stood around in my underpants.

He found another bush jacket and offered a three-carat deep blue sapphire I'd been admiring in the store. I couldn't argue with much confidence in my underpants and we made another deal.

He went back to his store wearing the original $20 suit from Mr. Minh's, which fitted him almost perfectly, and his staff clapped him and oohed and aahed as he priouetted amongst his hoard of sparkling gems.

"When you come back," he said, "bring more suits."

Marie made sure I did. Every time she packed my bags for Sri Lanka they were strangely overstuffed with my good suits.

"You don't want this old thing," she would say. "It's the wrong color anyway. And would you tell that poor man with the sapphires I want a big one that will look good by itself in a claw setting."

Marie would take the results of these suit swaps, and the lesser sapphires I picked up in the streets of Sri Lanka, to a Mr. Wong, a Hong Kong jeweler, to whom she had originally presented an ugly gold thing, with two artificial teeth in it, that a dentist had made for me years before to cure an overbite or something. Between them they produced what seemed to me to be an almost continual flow of exquisite rings and other pieces.

When the conference ended after a few weeks of violent anti-Western diatribe, I swapped my favorite light blue Mr. Ming bushjacket suit for a nineteen-carat sapphire of about the same color, and therefore not as valuable as the size indicates, and moved on to the Indonesian capital of Djakarta to pick up the Canadian group.

It was a good group, flying in a comfortable

Canadian Armed Services 707, with a perpetually open bar at the back, and it included many old friends from Ottawa days.

While Maceachen was busy being a statesman I took some of the reporters to see the story of the ordinary people of Djakarta, which is the story of the world. The story is on the banks of the river which flows through the city. There thousands of families, tens of thousands of people, live in extreme poverty in little temporary shacks built from junk. They wash, drink and empty their bowels in the thin trickle of water that flows in the middle of this wide, dry, dusty gulch. They have been driven to the city by rural poverty and the hope of at least survival, if not riches. But they haven't quite made it. Every now and then bulldozers and police with sledgehammers are sent by the city authorities to break down the shacks and push the people back. Then they begin creeping up on the city again.

From their hovels in the river these poor people can see and contemplate the modern streets of Djakarta only a few hundred yards away, with the steel and glass skyscrapers, the president's palace, the rich villas, and the hundreds of Mercedes limousines driven by the chauffeurs of the corrupt politicians, businessmen and generals. Djakarta had a population of only about 300,000 in 1945, almost six million now, and a predicted population of more than eighteen million by the year 2000.

They are nice people, these poor people, some of them educated enough to speak English, and they are the story in capsule of the world's urban crisis, of the increasing Third World demand for a new economic order, and of the world's potential for ugly revolution.

Even the good politicians like Maceachen don't have time to see these things; they see the chandeliered rooms of the embassy residences and the palaces of leaders. Maceachen spent much of his time in the palace of President Suharto, whose charming wife, Madame Tien, is notoriously rich and blatantly corrupt. The people who live in the river call her Madame Tien Percent.

We had a rest night in Bali and moved on to New Zealand for almost a week. A British journalist once led a story with the statement: "I visited New Zealand for a week but it was closed." It wasn't quite that bad when we were there, but we did go to a restaurant in Wellington one afternoon at about two o'clock and found it labeled "closed for lunch."

In Australia some of us interviewed the new prime minister, Malcolm Fraser, on his farm in Victoria and then flew to Canberra to cover Maceachen's official business. And that night the phone began to ring.

Australian Associated Press read me a wire instructing me to go to South Africa immediately. I'd been about six weeks on the road by now and I was tired. There was nothing I could do until morning so I went back to sleep. Reuters called a few minutes later with the same wire. Then after maybe an hour our Australian stringer called. Finally Mike Pieri, the *Star*'s new, young foreign editor, called to say I had to cover the riots then erupting between the Coloreds and Whites in Capetown.

"I don't have a work permit," I told Pieri sleepily. "You have to have a work permit to file from South Africa. Otherwise the big, white cops hit you on the head with billies or they throw you in jail. It's George Bain's beat. Why don't you send George?" Bain was our London correspondent.

"We can't send Bain," Pieri shouted over a fuzzy connection. "He doesn't have a work permit."

"That's what *I'm* saying," I yelled. "*I* don't have a work permit."

"Doesn't seem to matter," he said. "It's an order

188

from on high. The brass told me to send you to South Africa."

It didn't make any sense. I hung up and went back to sleep.

Gerald Long, the managing director of Reuters, made a speech to a meeting of the International Press Institute in Oslo in June, 1977. He said that although foreign correspondents are often thought to live lives of glamorous travel, unlimited expense accounts, partying with the famous, the reality is quite different. Foreign correspondents now live with more danger and harassment than at any time since World War II. He mentioned eighty-one cases of harassment and ill-treatment of foreign correspondents in a fourteen-month period and said: "Indications are that the foreign correspondent of the twentieth century is very much an endangered species."

Mr. Long had been responsible for the work of one of the largest and best teams of correspondents in the world for almost fifteen years and he knew what he was talking about. But in the newspaper offices, pressured by daily deadlines, plagued by excessive bureaucratic ambitions, afflicted by executive decisions made by committees and therefore often dangerously late, there was not a great deal of thought given to his warning.

In the newspaper offices somebody makes a decision, possibly somebody who has never been abroad and almost certainly somebody who believes abroad means London or Paris and that the Third World is somewhere on another planet altogether. The bureaucratic machine reacts to the instruction without a great deal of thought or understanding, except perhaps by the foreign editor, who understands, at least from reading the wires, the problems that might occur. But he possesses comparatively small authority and in the

189

end the correspondent has to sort it all out one way or another.

There is not even a real understanding of the fact that more than half the world is closed to the journalist although it is, in general, open to the businessman or even the tourist. Businessmen and tourists bring money. Journalists bring questions. Nothing in the passport arrangements between countries provides for this discrimination against journalists unless it is under a *Catch 22* phrase concerning the inadmissibility of undesirables. Still the foreign correspondent is regarded almost everywhere as a different breed from his fellow men and dangerous. At most of the world's airports now he is hustled aside and if he is not what the Chinese call a "friendly personage," usually an academic with a built-in bias posing as a journalist, he is tossed in jail, tortured, or worse. He is indeed an endangered species who will one day soon startle indifferent employers by asking for discrimination money in his contract because his profession cuts him off from such a huge part of the world he lives in, as if he suffers perpetual smallpox.

There are ways, of course, to beat the bureaucracies but they are becoming more difficult as the bureaucracies at home get bigger and more dangerous and as the bureaucrats abroad become more isolationist and more aware of the tricks a correspondent can play. One absolute necessity is to carry a large batch of blank letterhead paper from head office which can be filled in to fit any unpredictable complications.

Very often, when a correspondent does get into a country, he is asked for something weird, like a letter from his head office personally addressed to the deputy head of the telecommunications office, whose name is unpronounceable, and of course unpredictable, promising that wire transmission costs will be paid in *piastres* or *dong* or *baht* or whatever. Or he is asked to produce a declaration from his editors that he will submit his copy to a certain censor, who must be named; or a letter of introduction to the president of the country, who might have been an unknown sergeant before the coup of the previous week; or a guarantee from the head office that it will be responsible if the correspondent molests any local women or gets drunk on the local drink.

No real problem. The correspondent always has just such a letter back in his hotel room which he'll produce next time he comes to the ministry of information. For the sake of consistency I always used the forged signature of Mark Harrison, partly because his title of executive editor of *The Toronto Star* seemed to impress people, although it was in fact meaningless in the *Star* hierarchy, and partly because Mark was a former foreign correspondent who would understand. Marie would pre-sign the blank letterheads she put in my baggage and Mark became an authorizer and introducer all over Asia for activities and entrées he wouldn't care to contemplate.

Sometimes, though, a really blank letterhead was better than a genuine, Marie-signed Mark Harrison. Twice in Vietnam and once in India, when lowly bureaucrats blocked my journalistic way because I did not have the ever-necessary letter of introduction, I produced a blank letterhead and wrote, in front of them, in big print: "This is a letter of introduction," and I signed it myself. They let me pass.

The South African bureaucracy is a great deal more sophisticated than the often corrupt and usually inefficient Asian variety, however, and its secret service, The Bureau of State Security (BOSS) is an organization to be regarded with respect, awe, and fear.

When I woke up in Canberra, after the series of

191

messages from Canada, I told my colleagues I had to go to South Africa without a work permit and they told me I was stupid. But they were just a little envious. We complain often in the newspaper business about its stupidities, but it is still the excitement of the impossible assignment that gives the professional his kicks and these colleagues on this trip were professionals.

On the plane to Sydney that morning they helped me strip myself of anything that would identify me in any way as a journalist—my typewriter and camera, press passes, and accreditations. Reluctantly, as they checked me over, I gave them Marie's nineteen-carat sapphire in case I was hauled in as a smuggler.

We discussed whether the South African immigration entry card had a space where profession had to be noted. I couldn't remember from a previous visit, but I presumed it did. They all do. One old friend suggested I should give my profession as fabricator.

But the main problem was my passport. The Canadian government can be good to foreign correspondents if it thinks they are reliable and I had two passports, one for general purposes and one for difficult countries. The Canadian High Commission in Hong Kong took possession of one while I was using the other. It saved a lot of hassles. But on this trip I was carrying my favorite general-purpose passport which was absolutely full of visas and which I had foolishly not replaced for sentimental reasons. Instead Canadian embassies had glued inserts of additional pages in it. It was almost half an inch thick and when I produced it at airports the visa-packed pages fell out in a confusing concertina. It was not the passport of a businessman or tourist and was bound to attract special attention.

It was Sunday, but Maceachen's staff agreed to fix this up. They ordered a nice official named Miss Lyons away from her golf game to open the Sydney consulate. After all Macheachen was the minister of external affairs. And she gave me an absolutely pristine passport that didn't even show an arrival in Australia.

I changed from bush jacket into business suit and I took a first class flight to Johannesburg that night at the beginning of September, 1976. We are supposed to travel first class only in emergencies and I was anticipating an emergency. I waited until the economy class was booked and then bought my ticket.

When immigration cards were passed round the plane for us to fill out I gave my profession as company representative. The immigration desk at Johannesburg passed me through without a question. I caught a plane to Capetown and took a taxi to the middle of a riot.

Groups of young Cape Coloreds were roaming the streets of the warm, otherwise pleasant city, throwing stones, smashing the windows of cars and overturning them. Police riot squads, big white men in camoflaged battledress, where charging into the mobs, wielding billies and firing tear gas and shooting shotguns. Other police were using a harmless gadget called a thunder flasher which was intended to frighten the youngsters. It made a noice like an artillery barrage and it frightened me.

All of the downtown core of the city was in chaos. With Peter Younghusband, the *Star*'s stringer and one of the world's best correspondents, I made my way warily to the city hall square where hundreds of young Coloreds, their skins almost as white as ours, were rampaging. We were met by a barrage of big stones and flying pieces of debris and had to run. But from behind a wall we watched big white policemen charge into the mob, pistols drawn, swinging their sticks. Eventually they broke it up with tear gas.

As I wrote my story in Younghusband's office on the second floor of a building on the main St. George's

Street, I could see panicky mobs running through the street below, whites tripping over each other and knocking over parked motorcycles and bicycles as they fled from the scene of yet another disturbance. The sound of shotguns reverberated through the canyon of buildings, interspersed with the awful noise of the thunder flashers, making the riot sound like a war. Tear gas seeped somehow through the closed windows of the second storey office and my eyes watered so that I couldn't see the keys of the typewriter.

In South Africa you file your stories through a man named Fingers. He was a teletype operator, nicknamed for his prodigious speed on the keyboard, who anticipated the world communications revolution, the slowness of the official systems to react to it, and the world's interest in his country, and became a millionaire by supplying a fast and highly efficient service for correspondents.

Fingers will handle your copy at any time of the day or night or if he is not available Mrs. Fingers will do it. The copy goes through cleanly, but it is obvious that BOSS, the security agency, has a close eye on it and keeps its own copies for the record.

In recognition of this I added a note to this first story addressed to Pieri, the foreign editor, stating that I had arrived in Capetown on holiday as planned and found myself in the middle of a riot, so I'd filed a story just in case he wanted it. I was going to continue my holiday next day in the vineyard areas of the Cape, the note said.

Pieri wired back almost immediately apologizing profusely for interfering with my holiday plans and asking if I would remain in Capetown for just a few days in case there was any more trouble.

I covered the riots for ten days. About fifty people were killed and a thousand injured. Streets in the Black and Colored ghettos were burned out. The night sky glowed with the burning tires of street barricades and daytime visits to the settlements were nerve wracking experiences as the inhabitants glowered and growled at us, carrying stones, until we convinced them we were friends. Henry Kissinger, the U.S. Secretary of State, was on his shuttle through southern Africa at this time, seeking a solution to the Rhodesia crisis and conferring with the South African prime minister, thus guaranteeing a page one play a day, usually the main headline, even when the rioting was quiet.

All of my colleagues, including some who could be considered opposition journalists, knew I didn't have a work permit, but none of them gave me away. When I was sharing a car with some of them in the riot areas, they would often miss stories themselves by carefully avoiding situations in which we might be stopped by the police and asked for identification. One of them, Bruce Loudon, of the London *Daily Telegraph* was especially helpful although his paper was demanding stories of the "I was caught in a riot and hassled by the cruel cops" variety, even though the cops weren't necessarily cruel, just tough, really tough. Loudon knew how I felt. On one of his last few assignments he had been thrown in jail in Lusaka, in a cell with six people and three bunks, an experience he described in his British way as "awfully unpleasant, old chap."

After almost every story I filed I added another note complaining more and more bitterly about the interference with and finally the complete ruination of my holiday. I pointed out I was supposed to be having a well-earned rest after a long time on the road. I demanded double-time pay (although correspondents never receive such consideration while deskmen and reporters working in the comforts of the home office do). And I nagged away at Pieri about my great interest in wines, that I probably wouldn't have a chance again to see the vineyards of the Cape, and my great desire to see the rugby games between South Africa and New Zealand, the other main purpose of my visit. In the end I threatened to quit.

The young foreign editor replied with considerable skill, always apologetic, always asking for just one more day, just one more story, insisting that surely the authorities of a great country like South Africa would understand. After all, what was occurring, particularly at the meetings between Kissinger and the prime minister, was important to the world, and South Africa was not one of those banana republics, was it?

When the story was dying a little I decided I'd better give myself up before I was caught. Ten days of headlines in the *Star* had to have come to the attention of at least the South African Embassy in Ottawa, even in the unlikely event that the copy and the pained notes of distress had not been monitored on Finger's communications system by BOSS.

I made an appointment with a Mr. Traut, the official at the department of the interior who was in charge of work permits, and I entered his office with what I hoped was a look of frustration on my face.

He was a dour-looking man with an Africkaans accent.

"Would you do me a favor?" I asked after he'd sat me down. "Would you kick me out of your country?"

He leaned back in his chair looking surprised.

"I work for a newspaper, *The Toronto Star* in Canada," I explained. "I came here on a holiday. I wanted to tour the vineyards because I'm a bit of a wine buff and I'm very fond of South African wine. I wanted to see the rugby tests because I used to play rugby. I needed a break. But my bloody office in Canada keeps insisting that I write stories. I've told them you can't work here without a permit. They don't seem to understand and they keep asking me for just one more story and then another.

"I'm sick and tired of the whole thing," I said. "I've missed the rugby games anyway and I want to go home to my wife and kids in Hong Kong. Would you kick me out so I can go home?" I showed him copies of the exchange of notes between Pieri and me and a Mark Harrison letter telling me to enjoy my holiday. He turned out to be a nice man and he clucked his tongue in what I hoped was sympathy as he read the letter and my angry notes. We talked wine and rugby for a while. Then he said my request was an unusual case which would have to be considered in Johannesburg or Pretoria and I'd hear from him in a day or two.

He phoned in a few days and said there was just one problem. Would I write a letter to the department explaining why I had given my profession as company representative when I entered the country. He sounded stern.

I took some time composing the letter. I explained that I was, in fact, my company's representative in Asia and registered in Hong Kong for tax purposes and residence as the company representative. An alternative description could have been bureau chief, but experience had taught me nobody knew what this meant and it created confusion.

"A major part, although by no means all, of my duties in Asia are journalistic," I wrote. "But it is my custom when traveling on nonjournalistic duties or on a holiday to wear the other hat and use the term company representative. It saves unnecessary delays at airports and is the accurate description."

A few days after I personally handed the letter to the man from the ministry, he called again and invited me to his office.

Bruce Loudon shook hands seriously, said it had

# CHAPTER 13

# The death truck in Dacca

When a correspondent comes in from the cold he suffers a considerable culture shock. The people he meets in the plush homes and the clean, wide, uncrowded streets of the North American city do not seem to be quite real. To begin with the people don't care. They are dancing in discos. They are watching a dreamland on television. They are complaining about the price of steak and the need for a two-car garage. They seem to think this is the way the world is and will always be.

Even the journalists, or many of them, are into the "me generation," breaking the cardinal rule by writing about themselves, as if their moods, their families, their personal problems are important. They are long on words and short on facts and many of the editors, gauging, with the help of pollsters, an isolationist, switched-off mood of the readers, are encouraging the ignorance, helping to create a dangerous illusion of an unreal world.

Mozzamal Haq is a real person who lives out there in the real world of Dacca, Bangladesh, and on the day

I met him he was driving the truck that picks up the dead bodies in the streets of his city.

This was November, 1974, just after a bad flood had wiped out the rice harvest and driven hundreds of thousands of starving people from their farms into Dacca. A lot of them were just sitting day after day dying in the old cavernous railway station. Others huddled in circles in market places where they thought some charitable food distribution might occur sometime, but it usually didn't, and some just walked the streets until their skinny legs gave out and they collapsed and died in front of your eyes.

All of this made Mozzamal Haq and his 2½-ton Japanese-made truck very busy because Dacca is a big city and people were dying in places scattered far apart, but on the day I traveled in the van with him he was genial and cheerful and in a way he was enjoying his job.

"I feel I am doing good," he said at one stage. "I can't feed them. I can't even feed myself properly. But I can help give the dead ones a decent Moslem burial.

"It is true that the children upset me," he said. "The children don't weigh anything at all. They are just bones so they are no trouble to pick up. But it is because they have seen nothing but starvation. That is what worries and upsets me."

Mozzamal worked for a Moslem charitable organization named *Anjuman Mifidual Islam* (Essential Society of Islam) and in the last two weeks he had picked up 327 people who had just dropped dead and whose bodies were unclaimed by relatives or friends.

My ride in his truck was worse than covering a war. There is sometimes reason and valor and human dignity even in wars. But this was a journey into continuing hopelessness, confusion, corruption, and frustration; past naked, dying little children with old, wrinkled skins; through streets where the dirt sidewalks are littered with horizontal human debris, men without an ounce of fat on their bodies, women with breasts like long empty sacks, lying there waiting to die; and some families, mostly big families, huddled around a tiny, single bowl of ugly, yellow rice liquid, their meal for the day or longer.

On the steps of the railway station there was a skinny little abandoned baby, wrapped in a sack, dying, and when we climbed down from the van of the truck some pedicab drivers led us to the steps and lifted the top layers of sacking to show the baby's face. It was the face of a very old man and there were flies on it. But Mozzamal shook his head at the pedicab drivers and spread his arms in a gesture of frustration. The baby was still alive so it was too soon yet for the truck.

In a street near the railway station a mother was holding a dead baby in her arms and we stopped to see if we could take it from her. But the baby had just died and the mother was wailing and weeping so that Mozzamal was unable to communicate with her. He made a note of the place in a little book so that he would find it later.

About three miles from the center of the city, in the district of Jatrabari, we picked up the body of a man even though the man's family was still with him. He had been there for a while and the family was quite calm now. The sons explained that they could not pay the 500 taka ($62) cost of a funeral and they helped bundle their father into the back of Mozzamal's truck. He was an older man, perhaps fifty, so it was not all that bad. The widow just stood in silence, with her head bowed, as we drove away.

At Tangi, on the outskirts of the city, there were two little children lying dead beside the road and a woman was burning joss sticks near their heads. It was hard to tell whether the woman was the mother or grandmother or just someone who found the children

201

—at this time some young women in the streets of Dacca looked very old. There seemed to be no grief left in this woman with the dead babies' bodies and the joss sticks burning. We put the babies in the back with the old man and the woman said nothing.

On the way to the cemetery we stopped for a while at a kitchen in the working-class district of Malibagh, one of many such places set up by the Bangladesh government in an attempt to stem at least temporarily the tide of starvation deaths.

About 500 men, women, and little skinny children, naked or in rags, were squatting in orderly lines in silence, waiting for the handout from government workers. They had been there for many hours and they showed no reaction at all to the presence of Mozzamal and me and the death truck.

The government workers carried bamboo poles to beat back anyone who tried to get more than the ration, which was one thin bread wafer, called a *rooti*, per adult per day and one between two children.

As the workers went along the line old bony hands and the tiny hands of children clutched pathetically and the workers hit them with the bamboo poles in an attempt at orderliness.

Then when only about half the crowd had received a ration, the rootis ran out. The workers threw the last few into the air and there was a wild scramble for them in the dirt and then a near-riot as the unfed jostled with those who had food. The unfed children wailed and the workers wielded their poles among the scuffling, scrambling adults and then it was all over and the people went away somewhere, some of them to die.

At the cemetery on the outskirts of the city the bodies we had collected were washed and each was wrapped in a cheap, white burial robe called a *kafan*.

An *iman* (priest) read the *janaja* (last rites) and they were buried without coffins in shallow graves.

It cost the Essential Society of Islam 182 taka (about twenty-three dollars) to collect and bury each of the bodies. The *kafan* robe was the most expensive item at sixty taka ($7.50). Rosewater, camphor, soap, and incense cost twenty taka ($2.50) and the man who washed the bodies got five taka (sixty-two cents) a time. Gas and oil for Mozzamal's truck cost about fifty taka ($6.25) a body.

Mozzamal did not take his truck into the driveway of the luxurious Dacca Intercontinental Hotel, where the Westerners live, because he thought some of the guests might be offended by it. Instead he dropped me off down the road a bit.

I had a shower when I got to my room, poured a double scotch on the rocks and ordered a pepper steak and some Burgundy from room service. I was hungry but when the steak came I couldn't eat it.

When a correspondent comes home his memories are a kaleidoscope of colorful confusion, of wars and riots, hunger and horror, mixed here and there with some great acts of bravery and humanity, and even a little hope and happiness. He comes from a world in revolution, economically and politically, with refugees risking voyages in little leaky boats that make Captain Bligh's Pacific adventure look like a cruise in comparison; poor, confused, people migrating in millions away from oppression and starvation to somewhere else, almost anywhere else, where life is bound, they believe, to be better than it was.

The world the journalist leaves is in a state of demographic upheaval, of rapidly increasing education and expectations, of ancient tribal loyalties and love of national traditions mixed with an urgent desire to advance into the age of comfort and computers. In the circumstances, only one thing is uppermost in a reporter's mind, trained to zoom in on the main point, to spew out the essential simplicity of the story on deadline.

The basic simplicity is a bunch of statistics: the twenty most advanced industrial nations of the world comprise twenty percent of the world's population. They consume eighty percent of the world's goods. Close to half of the other 3.2 billion human beings on the earth live in desperate circumstances, earning less than $200 per capita per year.

About 900 million people live on or just over the fringe of starvation, in a condition, according to World Bank President Robert McNamara, "so limited by illiteracy, malnutrition, disease, high infant mortality, and low life expectancy as to deny its victims the very potential of the genes with which they are born."

But few people in North America—or Britain or Australia or Norway—are much interested in these statistics. These hungry people are far away, of no immediate consequence. The situation must be described another way. There are only 280 million people in North America, a mere twenty-three million in Canada. India's population is increasing by one Australia—thirteen million—a year. The Chinese make up a quarter of the entire population of the world and they intend to become an industrialized nation by the end of the century. Unless there is some sort of nuclear holocaust or horrible plague, the population of the world will double to eight billion before the present generation passes on.

Even the media, which publishes statistics about everything from unemployment to ball games, treats this granddaddy of all statistics with casual disrespect. Yet it is mainly the media, with its recent huge technological advances, that has advised the other people of the world of the way life *can* be and the power they have to achieve it. The media has made the statistic come alive and made it dangerous.

It is true that many of the 600 million people of India are still too poor to own radios, but they gather in hordes around the community set in their village at night to have the news explained by the village elder. The natives of New Guinea, who were still being enticed from the jungles by gifts of the white man's magical mirrors or steel axes when I first covered their primitive land in the 1950s, had transistor radios in their straw and mud houses on stilts when I returned in the seventies. The Vietnamese still tune surreptitiously to the BBC when they end their labors in the paddy fields of the New Economic Zones. A large number, if not a majority, of the people of Asia and Africa already have access to television. Because of the communications revolution, the Arabs of the deserts now know the value of oil. The skinny man working hard in the plantations of South America has heard the word about the outside world. He has used his knowledge to help create the new price of coffee.

The people who have fled in their hundreds of thousands from the continuing horror of Cambodia ever since Marie and I interviewed the first wave of them at Aranyapathet, still dropping dead by the thousands on the way to Thailand, are not stupid people despite the cruel Khmer regime's closure of schools and control of all information. Many are better educated than most in the West. Literacy rates all over Asia are high now, over seventy percent of the population in a majority of the countries, ninety-five percent in China, fifty-six percent among Indonesia's huge population of 136 million, even thirty percent in less advanced countries like Laos.

Some westerners claimed during Mrs. Gandhi's Emergency in India that she was right because a country of illiterates needed strong leadership. The literacy rate in India is now thirty-six percent. That's 227,880,000 educated Indians.

To be among the minority of illiterates doesn't mean to be stupid. It means a man can't read or write. It has nothing to do with wisdom or experience. The illiterate can also see, listen, and understand. He can hear the radio. He can watch the TV. He can think.

The phenomenon is new. Never before has the combination of increasing education and amazing communications technology so vividly informed the sufferers of the world of the extent of their misery and of the means available, military and moral, to overcome the extreme disparities between rich and poor, comfortable and starving. The rich ignore the poor but the poor are watching the rich.

So when a correspondent comes home to the comfortable world he misses the reality of the death truck in Dacca, the crowded masses, the kids crapping in the streets, the old, unliberated ladies up to their hips in mud behind the water buffalos, the queues of patient people outside the empty rice stores, the hordes of slum dwellers in the Djakarta river, creeping slowly and determinedly toward the riches of the city, and he remembers the words of the eighteenth century philosopher Chateaubriand:

"Try to convince the poor man, once he has learned to read and ceased to believe, once he has become as well informed as yourself, try to convince him that he must submit to every form of privation while his neighbor possesses a thousand times what he needs; in the last resort you would have to kill him."

In 1979 there were 2.529 billion people on the beat I covered in Asia alone. They have learned or are learning to read. Many of those who are not still brainwashed by tyrannical control of the flow of information, or dead or starving in countries controlled by the mad idealogues, are as well informed already as we are in the West.

We can try to switch them off as if their world is of no interest or consequence to us. But the switch won't work. They are still there. They won't go away.